Nobody's Perfect

A comedy

Simon Williams

Samuel French — London
New York - Toronto - Hollywood

NOBODY'S PERFECT

First presented by Jill Freud and Company at the Aldeburgh
Summer Theatre, Suffolk, in 1998 with the following
cast:

Leonard	Brian Mitchell
Harriet	Erika Hoffman
Dee Dee	Amy Williams
Gus	Stephen Hancock
Willie Briggs	Richard Magrin

Directed by **Alister Cameron**
Designed by **Maurice Rubens**

First presented in this revised version by Paul Farrah at the
Yvonne Arnaud Theatre, Guildford, in May 2001, and
subsequently on tour, with the following cast:

Leonard	Simon Williams
Harriet	Stephanie Beacham
Dee Dee	Amy Williams
Gus	Moray Watson

Directed by **Andy de la Tour**
Designed by **Julie Godfrey**

CHARACTERS

Leonard, a statistician, middle-aged
Harriet, a publisher
Dee Dee, Leonard's daughter
Gus, Leonard's father
Willie Briggs, a passer-by, any age (non-speaking)

The action of the play takes place in a south-west London
flat and in a central London publishing house

Time: the present. Autumn

ACT I

A flat in south-west London and an office in a London publishing house. It is autumn

The set is a composite. DR *is part of the street, a lamp-post and the front door, possibly up a few steps, to the block of flats, one of which is the main set. By the front door is an entryphone with a handset. The principal acting area is a basement flat. The living-room is fairly well lived-in and modern. There is an entryphone with a handset here, too. It is obvious from the desk, computer, fax, intercom system, cordless phone, etc. that this is a place of work. The desk also holds a transistor radio. Up stage a hall leads to the bedrooms and bathroom.* DL *is the third separate acting area: the office of a magazine editor. There are wall charts round the desk which is tidy and business-like*

As the CURTAIN *rises, Harriet is in the editor's office reading from a distinctive-looking manuscript bound in turquoise*

Harriet (*reading to herself*) "...Daphne's heart was pounding as Alfonso carried her down the narrow cliff path..." Uh-ho, not another orgasm on the beach... (*She turns the pages*) Yeah, yeah, yeah. "Alfonso slipped his wicked Italian fingers under Daphne's turquoise satin blouse. 'I want you, Bellissima, I want you here—I want you now...' I want you in the waste paper basket. (*She bins it*) I just hate turquoise. Plus I bet it's written by a bloke. (*She reads as she types a letter*) "Dear Colonel Truscott, thank you for submitting the first chapter of your manuscript... *Gone With The Window Cleaner* which I am returning..."

The Lights cross-fade as Leonard enters the flat, carrying the distinctive-looking manuscript. He is wearing rubber gloves and an apron and reading the letter out loud

Leonard "...We did stipulate in the rules for the competition that we were looking for romantic fiction from first-time female writers... Unless I'm very much mistaken you also submitted a very sub-standard manuscript called *Sleepless In Bootle*. Same style, different pen-name." (*He growls*) "...Love Is All Around is a feminist publishing house. Our readers want heroines of today written by women of today who really understand the lonely struggle of daily life as a working parent. Don't mess with me, Colonel Truscott or whoever you are. With good wishes, Harriet Copeland. (*He drops the manuscript in the waste paper basket. To himself*) What do you know, Miss Harriet Copeland, what do you know about the lonely struggle of daily life as a working parent. I'll show you. (*He sits at his laptop and takes off his gloves*) "Emily peeled off her Marigolds with grim determination. 'I've had enough of all this gender bias,' she thought, 'I just want to be judged as a person.' (*He rises*) 'As a woman of today…'" (*He stops inspired and then types*) *Meet Me In St Albans* by Myrtle Banbury…

Leonard exits as we cross-fade to Harriet's office

Harriet (*with Leonard*) *Meet Me In St Albans* by Myrtle Banbury——

The phone rings. She answers it

Hallo. Love Is All Around. Harriet Copeland… Hi Lindsay. … Not at all, I need distraction, I'm up to my ears in sex. … Yes, right here all over the desk. Come on, Linds, you remember sex. … That's the one—like shopping without the sore feet. Join the club. … Huh? The all-men-are-complete-and-utter-bastards club… He's dumped me. … What? Actually he was nigh on perfect: five parts Mel Gibson, three parts Jeremy Paxman. … I'm just throwing myself into my work. … Pretty busy actually. We're desperate for new books, that's why we're running this wretched competition. Don't knock it, I tell you there's big money in romantic fiction. The trouble is finding women who can write it without their tongue in their cheek. … Don't be filthy, Linds. There's a world of suckers out there who are still looking for happy endings. Most of the entries we've got here are either pathetic or pornographic. I've got one here… (*She picks it out of the pile and reads*) *Withering Tights*—it's about a randy little greengrocer who does things with vegetables that'd put you off ratatouille for life. … OK. I'll send you a copy. (*She hangs up and dumps the manuscript in the bin*) Where was I? (*She resumes*) This is actually rather good…

The Lights cross-fade to Leonard as he enters in an apron and puts the ironing on the landing chest. He then follows the actions described

(*Reading*) "Emily had finished all the ironing and left it neatly folded on the table. Wearily she took off and folded her apron… Her back ached with all the housework. She studied herself in the mirror…"

Leonard looks into the mirror on the fourth wall

"…a tired, unloved, middle-aged woman. She sighed wearily and then sat at her desk and sipped her coffee, staring bleakly into space. She was feeling that sudden awareness of loneliness that comes back uninvited at dusk. She didn't know that her life was about to change."

Leonard is now typing and reading

Leonard "Any minute now Emily's daughter would be home from school…"

At the front door Dee Dee arrives. She is wearing a Walkman and stubbing out a cigarette

Dee Dee acts accordingly as her father types and reads at his desk … she enters the building

"As always she would pause on the doorstep, stub out her illicit cigarette, wipe off her lipstick and give her mouth a quick squirt. Daddy's little…" Whoops. Delete. Delete. "Mummy's little girl…" Hang on…

Leonard rushes to the kitchen and returns with a can of Coke and a packet of crisps which he puts on the table

In the office:

Harriet (*reading*) I like this. A single mum who's really been there… Myrtle Banbury…

In the main set: still with her headset on, Dee Dee enters and follows the routine that her father reads out as he types

Leonard (*reading and typing*) "In she'd come…"

The front door slams

"…and without taking her Walkman off, she'd dump all her stuff in the middle of the floor, kick her shoes off in opposite directions, grab a Coke and some crisps and stomp off to her room to watch *Neighbours*…"

Having picked up the Coke and crisps, Dee Dee, after a weary look at her dad, exits to her bedroom

(*Turning to her and shouting*) Just don't let me catch you finishing your essay, my girl. And the door slams…

The door slams

There we are.

Leonard continues typing and miming, while in the office Harriet reads

Harriet (*reading*) "What would Trevor be like, Emily wondered. Blind
dates weren't really her thing, but…
Leonard (*with relish*) "…as a single parent facing the lonely struggle of
daily life…"
Harriet "She didn't suppose she had much choice."

Leonard runs his fingers through his hair

"She'd have to wash her hair; would she wear it up or down…? And…"

Leonard looks at his nails

"…her nails. She'd have to paint her nails… Red? Coral…?"

Leonard ⎫
                  ⎬ (*together*) "Peach."
Harriet ⎭
Harriet Now here's a woman after my own heart. This is the real McCoy—
I can spot a fake at ten pages. (*She checks the name and picks up the
manuscript*) Come on, Myrtle Banbury, I'm taking you home…

Harriet picks her stuff and exits

*Dee Dee enters the living-room, still wearing the headset and heading for
the kitchen*

*Leonard waves at her and mouths something deliberately indiscernible to
her. Dee Dee reluctantly takes off her headset*

Dee Dee (*crossly*) What?
Leonard Nothing. Got you, though.

Dee Dee lets out a huge groan

How was school?
Dee Dee Gross.
Leonard Was Justin there? How was he?
Dee Dee Gross.

Leonard And you missed your bus and got caught in the rain and you left your lunch on the hall table. All in all pretty...
Dee Dee Gross.
Leonard Well, it's good to see you, my little ray of sunshine.

Dee Dee groans

You know when you've got twelve dozen of something—what's it called?
Dee Dee What?
Leonard Twelve dozen of something is a...?
Dee Dee What?
Leonard Gross. It's a gross... Joke.
Dee Dee Pathetic. When I come home from that cruddy effing school I don't want to talk about Justin Effing Barrett and I don't want to have to put up with you being a game show host.
Leonard Sorry, sorry. Point taken.

A beat

I am the weakest link. Goodbye.
Dee Dee You're a pain, you know that.
Leonard A sharp stabbing one or a dull ache. That's the trouble with being a statistician.
Dee Dee What?
Leonard Ninety-one-point-five per cent of us are a pain.
Dee Dee Why can't you be more like Grampi?
Leonard Because basically I'm a decent, honest, clean, punctual, tidy human being.
Dee Dee If you send him back to that retirement home I'll never speak to you again.
Leonard That's a threat I may have to live with. He can't stay here for ever.
Dee Dee You are so not nice.
Leonard You mean not so nice.
Dee Dee Horrid.
Leonard You know, I think you were born frowning—I remember the midwife saying "Oh Mr Loftus. It's a bonny wee girl." And I thought "No, it's not, it's a furious little gerbil." I've got albums full of you scowling away. (*Sweetly*) Come on, Dee Dee... Say cheese for Daddy. (*Brutally*) Wensleydale.
Dee Dee Poor old Dad, what you wanted was Shirley Temple.
Leonard Yeah, and I ended up with Ann Widdecombe.
Dee Dee You just don't understand women.
Leonard Oh, is that the trouble?

Dee Dee All you do is annoy them.

Leonard So it seems. But you're a person, remember, not a girl when it comes to tidying her room.

Dee Dee No. Hang on—what I said was room tidying is not a gender issue.

Leonard Oh, pardon me.

Dee Dee It's my room.

Leonard It's my flat.

Dee Dee It's my mess.

Leonard You're my daughter... Whoops, offspring.

Dee Dee I've had enough of this.

Leonard I'm sorry—come and give me a kiss.

Dee Dee You only want to see if I smell of cigarettes.

Leonard I'll hold my nose. Give me a hug.

Dee Dee I'm in a bad mood.

Leonard Surely not.

Dee Dee There you go again. I mean why do you always have to make sarcastic little jokes when we're having a row, why can't you fly off the handle and wag your finger and stuff like a normal father.

Leonard (*wagging his finger*) Come here this minute and hug your father.

She goes to him

I'm sorry I annoy you, it's a special knack I have with women. It's taken years of practice.

Dee Dee Is that why Mum left you, do you think?

Leonard Yup. She told me I was the most irritating man in the whole of Surrey... But I said with a population of two-point-three million that that was statistically improbable.

Dee Dee And what did she say?

Leonard She threw a jar of bolognese sauce at me. Once, you know, she even said she hated my hairbrush.

Dee Dee Your hairbrush?

Leonard Hmm. I mean, it's a perfectly ordinary hairbrush.

Dee Dee So her leaving you, had nothing to do with that nerd she ran off with.

Leonard No.

Dee Dee The Porsche, the Giorgio Armani, the Paco Rabanne...

Leonard Had nothing to do with it.

Dee Dee Oh, come on.

Leonard Well, all right then, maybe just a teensy weensy little ninety-nine-point-nine per cent.

Dee Dee Exactly.

Leonard No, it was my fault really—as you said I don't know much about women. When we were first married I thought PMT was a kind of pension fund. I've never been any good at that side of things.

Dee Dee What? What side of things?

Leonard S-E-X.

Dee Dee We all know how to spell it, Dad. Say it.

Leonard No.

Dee Dee Go on.

Leonard No.

Dee Dee (*tickling or punching him*) Say it.

Leonard (*like Noël Coward*) Sex.

Dee Dee Bravo ... again.

Leonard No.

Dee Dee (*loudly*) SEX.

Leonard No.

Dee Dee Once a night enough for you, eh?

Leonard Dee Dee, don't be filthy.

Dee Dee I'm not being filthy. It's just that sometimes you have to say things, Dad. Some things need saying—out loud. Not whispered or mumbled or said in code.

Leonard You mean not in Eggy-Peggy?

Dee Dee Yes. Not in Eggy-Peggy. I think it's a bit of a cop-out. Emotionally.

Leonard Deggo yeggou?

Dee Dee Yes I do. I mean just try it, hmm? Say "I love you".

Leonard EggI Leggove Yeggou.

Dee Dee Not in Eggy-Peggy.

Leonard That's the way we've always done it. We've always spoken in Eggy-Peggy. You and I.

Dee Dee Oh Dad, why can't you loosen up.

Leonard Some knots are just tied too tight. You know me.

Dee Dee Yeah, as soon as you meet a pretty girl you go all stammery and blinking... (*Impersonating him*) H-h-hallo. I'm a boring old f-f-art.

Leonard You are horrible. (*He holds her in his arms*) I suppose if I did say your hair smelt of cigarettes you'd tell me it was the boy next to you in the bus shelter.

Dee Dee Of course. You do miss her though, don't you?

Leonard Your mum? Yes. I do.

Dee Dee Even after all this time?

Leonard Four years and two months.

Dee Dee There's never been anyone else, has there?

Leonard Well, every now and then Julia Roberts and I pop over to Paris for a dirty weekend.

Dee Dee In your dreams.

Leonard Of course... I suppose I'm a bit of a penguin really.

Dee Dee You like waddling around in the freezing cold eating raw fish?

Leonard They mate for life, apparently. For me it wasn't an open-ended kind of deal, falling in love. It was a one-off, once-in-a-lifetime thing, like having your appendix out, or meeting Noël Edmonds.

Dee Dee Poor old Dad. (*Being a penguin*) Isn't love a bummer? Honestly.

Leonard What do you mean?

Dee Dee Well, it's not the old fairy tale of hearts and flowers, is it? At the end of the day it's just a lot of hormones rampaging about, making you go do-lally. I mean, who needs it? Especially with a steaming great two-faced nerd like Justin Effing Barrett with his barmy sodding Ray-Bans. Him and his, "Get a grip, girl, heavy isn't cool". Who needs it?

Leonard Well, put like that I suppose none of us do. Chin up, I'll get us supper in a minute. It's chicken in mushroom——

Dee Dee ——sauce with broccoli and new potatoes.

Leonard Yes.

Dee Dee It's Wednesday, right?

Leonard Plus Grandpa is doing us one of his puddings.

Dee Dee Oh Lord, I've only just recovered from his Half Baked Alaska.

Leonard The man who brought road-rage to the Magimix. He says this one is called Dalmation Willy. A variation on Spotted Dick.

Dee Dee (*going to the stairs*) You see, that's where you get it from. You are going to let him stay, though, aren't you?

Leonard There's not room here for all three of us, my darling. He gets under my feet all day.

Dee Dee He's jolly useful.

Leonard Helping you with your essays and stuff, you mean?

Dee Dee You can't send him back to Birchampton, he's not ready for a retirement home.

Leonard They won't have him—not after the last incident.

Dee Dee goes to her room

What he needs is a Saga Borstal... He just wants to grow old disgracefully... Where was I? (*He returns to his computer*)

Dee Dee speaks on her intercom

Dee Dee (*off*) Hallo. Hallo... Wensleydale to Penguin. Hallo.

Leonard (*on the desk intercom*) Yup?

Dee Dee (*off*) I just wanted to say—speaking for myself—I'm really quite fond of your hairbrush.

Leonard (*on the desk intercom*) Are you? Well, I ... er ... er...

Dee Dee Love you too?

Leonard That's the one.

Leonard goes back to his writing

(*Writing and reading*) "Isn't love a bummer, Emily thought as she stared..."

Gus, Leonard's father, arrives at the front door. He is remarkably youthful and at ease, casually dressed (baseball cap etc.) and weighed down with shopping. He has obviously lost his key

"...into the blackness of Trevor's barmy sodding Ray-Bans. It's not at all the old fairy story of hearts and flowers, it's just a lot of hormones..."

Gus has no choice but ring the bell. Mid-flow, as a matter of habit, Leonard goes to the entryphone

(*Into the entryphone*) Top left inside pocket.
Gus (*immediately finding his keys*) Of course. Thank you...
Leonard (*returning to his desk*) "...rampaging about ... making you go do-lally... Who needs it, she thought..."

Gus presses the intercom again. And again Leonard has to go and answer it

Yes?
Gus You should have it printed for me on a card here next to the buzzer.
Leonard I did.
Gus Oh (*He peers at the buzzer*) Glasses...?
Leonard Inside breast pocket.
Gus (*finding them*) You're a lovely boy... You know sometimes I think I'm losing my mind.
Leonard That's probably in your trouser pocket.

Gus lets himself into the building; while he is out of view, Leonard goes back to the computer

"'Get a grip, girl' she told herself, 'getting heavy isn't cool.'"

The front door opens and Gus enters the flat

Gus Hallo there. You probably didn't want interrupting.
Leonard No.
Gus Is that "Good Heavens, no, perish the thought"?
Leonard No.
Gus Ah. It's "no, I do not want to be interrrupted".
Leonard Yes.
Gus Got it. What I should have said was: "Am I interrupting?"

Leonard Yes.

Gus It's not quite the same, is it? I mean I could have been interrupting and you *wanted* to be interrupted.

Leonard That was not the case.

Gus So you're busy.

Leonard No.

Gus No?

Leonard I *was* busy, but I've given up.

Gus Still working on the disposable nappies?

Leonard (*doing the commercial voice over*) Do you know what the great British public spends on disposable nappies per day, Dad? One million, two hundred and sixty thousand pounds.

Gus I feel deeply enriched by the knowledge.

Leonard ...That is because every day British women give birth to six and a half tons of new-born babies.

Gus I don't know what to say to that.

Leonard Have a drink?

Gus (*looking at his wrist*) That's not a bad idea.

Leonard I don't know why you bother looking at your watch.

Gus Actually I wasn't. (*He shows his wrist is bare*) I've mislaid it.

Leonard Bathroom shelf. You've probably been in *The Rose and Crown* all day.

Gus No, I have not.

Leonard I'm sorry.

Gus It was *The Rising Sun*, I had a couple of winners at Chepstow.

Leonard The bookies and the pub, you have been busy.

Gus And ten pounds on a scratchcard.

Leonard I thought you were going to give the Day Centre a try?

Gus I couldn't face it. There must be some better way of keeping out from under your feet for a few hours.

Leonard I'm sure you'll find it.

Gus I mean, I know I'm old, I have to shave this craggy old face every morning, but I'm not blind—well, only a bit. I don't feel old and I don't like old people. What exactly is lap-dancing, by the way?

Leonard Whatever it is, Dad, I don't reckon you'll find it at the Day Centre.

Gus Certainly not. What I need is a Charlie Dimmock look-a-like with a huge annuity and poor eye sight. All those whingeing old crones in pastel knitwear, that's not what I'm looking for.

Leonard What are you looking for, Dad?

Gus A wife.

Leonard You don't want a wife.

Gus No, of course not, but at my age and with my little problem I haven't got much to offer, have I?

Leonard Well, there's always your Baywatch posters and all your Pokémon cards. Anyway, what is your little problem?

Gus Never you mind. All I'm trying to say is I can't go on staying here. Indefinitely.

Leonard folds his arms and hums nonchalantly

...Can I?

Leonard I didn't say anything.

Gus Oh.

Leonard I thought it was a rhetorical question.

Gus It wasn't.

Leonard Oh... Well, no, you can't.

Gus What?

Leonard Stay here indefinitely.

Gus strikes a pathetically downcast pose with a little sob

And spare me the Steptoe impersonation.

Gus Oh, come on, you can't send me back to Birchampton.

Leonard No, I can't. They won't have you. You're the first person in thirty-seven years they've had to expel.

Gus Storm in a teacup.

Leonard Gross indecency.

Gus No, no, it was too cold for gross. Mild perhaps. It was a misunderstanding. Mrs Spenlow had told me she was having trouble with her appliance. I was trying to help.

Leonard You are quite incorrigible.

Gus It was a trumped-up charge, Lenny, I was framed.

Leonard For goodness sake—the woman in question was eighty-two.

Gus All right then, Zimmer-framed.

Leonard groans like Dee Dee

Silly old bat, even with her teeth out she was a fearful flirt... So you don't want me here?

Leonard (*delicately*) Not necessarily all the time. The flat isn't big enough for all three of us.

Gus Dee Dee will be off to University soon. You'll be lonely then.

Leonard (*seeing the truth of this*) Yes... But not that lonely. She says she caught you watching a young mother's aerobic class last week.

Gus Only in passing.

Leonard From the roof of Debenhams with my binoculars. You are a greedy scheming dirty old man.

Gus On a good day. The little stinker. (*Into the intercom to Dee Dee*) You're a horrible little sneak...

Dee Dee (*off; on the intercom*) Hi there, Grampi. Have you done my King Lear essay?

Gus (*into the intercom*) No, and any more grassing on me and I'll tell your Dad about your tattoo.

Leonard What tattoo? Where?

Dee Dee (*off*) None of your business.

Leonard Oh, no... Not there... Not on her... Not there.

Gus Well, at least you'll never see it.

Leonard What's it say?

Gus (*shaking his head*) Strictly private.

Leonard Tell me.

Gus That's what it says: "Strictly private".

Leonard You are a bad influence.

Gus How come then I sired you, Mr Squeaky Clean?

Leonard There's nothing wrong with being...

Gus What?

Leonard With being me... Am I really so boring?

Gus folds his arms and hums as Leonard did

Hm?

Gus I didn't say anything.

Leonard Oh.

Gus I thought it was a rhetorical question.

Leonard It wasn't.

Gus Well... Well, it's not that you're boring, it's just that you lead a boring life and that tends to make you...

Leonard Boring.

Gus (*tapping the computer*) You spend all day stuck in front of your Apple Mac. Staring at the screen. It's not healthy.

Leonard What do you mean?

Gus Well, how come you always shut it down when I come in, eh? You're not doing mucky things on the internet, are you?

Leonard No.

Gus It can't be good for you messing about with facts and figures.

Leonard It's my livelihood. There's nothing wrong with facts and figures.

Gus They are dull.

Leonard They are safe and solid.

Gus Get a life.

Leonard I've got one.

Gus Get another. Look, you're my only son and I love you, but there is a world out there, a living breathing utterly brilliant world you're missing out on, a world full of so many not boring things.

Leonard Name ten.

Gus Ten? I'll give you twenty: Guinness, Shakespeare, The Beatles, Yorkshire pudding, *The Archers*, Brenda Langton, *One Man and his Dog*...

Leonard can interrupt whenever, as long as Brenda Langton has been mentioned

Leonard OK. Point taken. So the world is passing me by—I can't help it.

Gus You can. You can. It's not too late.

Leonard It is, I'm afraid. Who is Brenda Langton?

Gus (*producing the spotted dick from one of his bags*) She's the buxom lady in *The Rising Sun* who helped me with the pudding I've made for this evening. All I'm saying is... Live a little dangerously. Leave the top off the toothpaste once in a while, wear a thong, say "bum" to a traffic warden.

Leonard I am perfectly happy as I am.

During the following, Dee Dee enters and listens to Gus with her mouth open

Gus You'll die of boredom. Get a life, dear boy, get down and get dirty, sock it to 'em, hang loose...

Dee Dee That's telling him, Grampi.

Gus Hallo, poppet.

Gus and Dee Dee kiss

Dee Dee I love it when you talk sixties.

Gus How's things?

Leonard Gross.

Dee Dee Fine. So what was all that about?

Leonard He wants to turn me into Peter Stringfellow.

Dee Dee You should listen to your father.

Leonard So should you. Is this a conspiracy?

A mobile phone rings in Gus's pocket. Gus is unaware. They all look for it

Dee Dee (*finding the mobile*) It's in your pocket, Grampi.

Leonard (*taking it and answering it*) Hallo? ... Mrs Duff? ... What? ... Who? ... Hold On. (*He covers the receiver, stalking Gus*) It's a Mrs Duff asking for the Earl of Loch Ness.

Gus Oh my God. (*He takes the mobile and speaks with a very bad broad Scottish accent*) Hallo, Mrs Duff? ... Och no, he is na here. ... I dinna ken... I'm just his gamekeeper.... Very well, Mrs Duff... I'll tell the Laird if he calls. (*He disconnects*)

Dee Dee Ooh Granpapa, what big teeth you've got.

Leonard So who is Mrs Duff?

Gus I met her at a Greenpeace disco last week. We had tea together and then she started getting rather heavy.

Leonard Too many scones. I've told you not to take my mobile—especially not for telling such porkies on.

Dee Dee (*looking into a bag*) What's all this in here, Grampi? (*She takes a dress*) You didn't take all her clothes, did you?

Leonard You didn't leave Mrs Duff in the buff, did you, Dad? Or are you a transvestite now?

Gus If you must know there's a group of us going on a murder weekend in Haywards Heath.

Leonard Clear off, both of you.

Dee Dee (*taking out a huge bra*) Sick, sick, sick. What's this?

Gus It's for the fuller-figured woman.

Dee Dee It's for the randy old goat.

Leonard And you're going as the Himalayas?

Gus Miss Marple actually. (*In a camp Lady Bracknell voice*) I thought to myself—I may not solve the murder but I'd have such fun in the dressing room.

Dee Dee and Gus pick up all the bags etc. and exit to the kitchen as Leonard starts typing again

Harriet enters her office

Leonard (*typing and reading*) "'There's a world out there, a living breathing utterly brilliant world you're missing out on...' Trevor leaned across the table towards Emily and whispered..."

Harriet is chuckling at the last paragraph she has read

Harriet "'Live a little dangerously...'" That's the stuff, Myrtle... (*She dials a number*) That's the kind of thing we need... I've had enough of nooky on the shagpile and shagging by the Inglenook.

The phone rings on Leonard's desk and he answers it

Leonard Hallo. (*He takes a sip of tea*)

Harriet I have that as the contact number for Myrtle Banbury.

Leonard (*spluttering*) What?

Harriet Myrtle Banbury. She's sent me the first chapter of a romantic novel called *Meet Me In St Albans*. Could I speak to her?

Leonard Speak. Speak to Myrtle Banbury...? In what way speak?

Harriet Speak ... as in oral communication... My name is Harriet Copeland, I work at Love Is All Around...

Leonard Love Is All Around...?

Harriet We've been running this competion to find new writers and I wanted to speak to Myrtle Banbury to tell her that she has been short-listed.

Leonard Short-listed...? (*He laughs idiotically*)

Harriet Are you all right?

Leonard Yes. No. I'm fine.

Harriet Now look, as I said I'm Harriet Copeland and you are ...

Leonard Yes, yes, I am.

Harriet Your name...

Leonard (*desperately seeking inspiration*) My name... Mac... Apple... MacApple... Mr MacApple... Stringfellow MacApple ... that's me... I'm nothing to do with anything.

Harriet Well, the thing is, Mr MacApple, I do have to talk to Myrtle Banbury, is she there?

Leonard Yes... No... Yes... No... Why?

Harriet I wanted to tell her in person, but she is in fact the winner.

Leonard The winner?

Harriet I need to discuss the deal with her.

Leonard The deal...?

Harriet As in money, Mr MacApple. It obviously involves rather large sums...

Leonard (*giggling in ecstasy*) Large sums... Tee-hee... Large sums... (*In his excitement he disconnnects by mistake*) Hallo. Hallo.

Harriet Hallo. Hallo.

Leonard Oh, blast.

Harriet I've got another nutter here.

Leonard (*imploring the phone*) Oh please, Miss Copeland, please press re-dial.

He gives up in despair and is going to replace the cordless phone when it suddenly rings in his hand. Leonard jumps and then answers it. He holds the phone at arm's length and shouts as if to someone in another room

Nurse, please restrain Mr MacApple... Stop biting my carpet, Mr MacApple... Nurse, please take Mr MacApple back to the hostel. Thank you, nurse. Bye bye, Mr MacApple... (*He sings a bit of nonsense as*

MacApple and then manages to reach and slam the front door as a sound effect. He puts the phone to his ear and resumes very smoothly) Hallo...

Harriet Hallo. Love Is All Around.

Leonard I'm so glad.

Harriet What is going on?

Leonard Poor old MacApple, he's a few marbles short of a picnic.

Harriet What? Who is he?

Leonard My father... No... He thinks he's my father... Poor old soul, there's a hostel next door, he has these delusions, he used to think he was Tarzan... Quite harmless really.

Harriet Quite, you don't see enough blokes in leopard-skin pants down at Tescos. So who am I talking to now?

Leonard *(smoothly)* My name is Leonard Loftus. Do I gather you want to publish *Meet Me in St Albans*?

Harriet Yes, I want to talk to Myrtle Banbury.

Leonard My aunt.

Harriet Your aunt?

Leonard Auntie Myrtle. I can't tell you how thrilled she'll be.

Harriet I want to talk to her—is that possible?

Leonard Is it possible for you to talk to Myrtle Banbury?

Harriet Yes.

Leonard No. She's incontinent. On the continent. On the contrary, she's out of the country... She's abroad.

Harriet What about you?

Leonard I'm still here.

Harriet You can reach her, though, can you?

Leonard Yes, yes, of course—I'll tell her all the details and then I'll call you back... How much?

Harriet You mean how much is the prize money? I should say altogether in the region of fifteen thousand pounds.

Leonard *(amazed)* Yes. Well, that is a very nice region. Fifteen thousand pounds. A very lovely region. One of her favourites.

Harriet There will of course be many other matters to work out, options and so forth, obviously.

Leonard Obviously. I'll be managing all her affairs—you can deal with me.

Harriet All the same, I really do need to speak to her, Mr Loftus. Where is she?

Leonard I'm afraid she's incommunicado. Disparu.

Harriet What?

Leonard Darkest Peru.

Harriet Please get her to call me.

Leonard I suppose a fax is out of the question?

Harriet I want to talk to her——

Leonard There's no signal…
Harriet —in person.
Leonard In person. Lovely. I'll see what I can do.
Harriet Goodbye for now then, Mr Loftus.
Leonard Goodbye.

Leonard and Harriet both hang up

Harriet What a nerd.

Harriet exits

Leonard What a cow.

Gus arrives at the front door

(*Distraught*) "Oh what a tangled web we weave…"

Dee Dee enters to return the mobile

Dee Dee "When first we practice to deceive…"

Leonard exits into the kitchen

On the other hand, practice makes perfect.

Gus presses the intercom and Dee Dee answers

Dee Dee Hullo…
Gus It's me. Are you alone?
Dee Dee (*checking*) Pretty much.
Gus I need money.
Dee Dee What for?
Gus A kind of debt… I was at this club.
Dee Dee What club?
Gus Lap dancing.
Dee Dee Oh Grampi.
Gus I thought it was a group thing and we all had to join in.
Dee Dee That's line dancing, for Heaven's sake.
Gus I thought she was just being friendly.
Dee Dee Who?
Gus Muriel. Lovely girl. A trainee dental hygienist.
Dee Dee How much?

Gus Twenty-eight quid.

Dee Dee Twenty-eight quid. That's friendly enough. Leave it with me, I'll see what I can do. (*She hangs up*)

Leonard enters

Hi, Dad. Are you OK?

Leonard No, I am not. I've got a bit of a problem.

Dee Dee Me too.

Leonard What's that, my darling?

Dee Dee Well... You know Rosalie Crabtree, my best friend at school... Well, she's been on this sponsored swim, you see.

Leonard What for?

Dee Dee What for...? Five p a length.

Leonard How many lengths did she do?

Dee Dee Five hundred and sixty.

Leonard My God, that's twenty-eight pounds.

Dee Dee Good Lord so it is. But it is for a good cause.

Leonard What?

Dee Dee Help The Aged.

Leonard (*giving her the money*) Well, there you are.

Dee Dee Thanks, Dad. Love you, love you, love you.

Dee Dee blows him a kiss and goes

Leonard Yeah yeah yeah... (*He picks up the mobile ... he puts it down ... he picks it up again. He tries the voice Gus used*) "I thought to myself I may not solve the murder but I'll have such fun in the dressing room..." (*He dithers*) No no no... Yes yes yes... (*He dials*)

Outside the front door Dee Dee is handing over the money to Gus

Dee Dee Here we are, Grampi...

Gus Come with me, poppet, she's waiting in the taxi round the corner... With her brothers.

Gus and Dee Dee exit

The phone rings in Harriet's office

Harriet enters to answer it

Harriet Hallo... Love Is All Around... Harriet Copeland... Hallo... Hallo...

Leonard holds the receiver away from him and makes static noises, firstly with his mouth and then with a transistor radio—he twiddles the dial to add to the noise of a great distance. Intermittently, Leonard croaks "Hallo... England?"

Hallo... Hallo...

With great trepidation Leonard starts his performance as Myrtle, he speaks into the receiver from arm's length

Leonard (*as a Spanish operator*) Hallo... Buenos tarde... Quiero hablar con Love Ith All Around... Inglaterra...? Si? Ith England, yeth? Ith Love Ith All Around, yeth?

Harriet Yeth. Yes. Is that Myrtle Banbury?

Leonard It is... It is... It's me, Myrtle Banbury. I'm so glad you like my little book.

Harriet Oh yes, very much. It was a clear winner—funny, touching— quintessentially feminine. Now, your nephew——

Leonard Dear Leonard, yes.

Harriet —told you the deal I had in mind?

Leonard Yes indeed. A lovely region. Most welcome. In fact I'd like you to let him have a ten per cent advance, in cash, as soon as possible.

Harriet Good. Now tell me are you still in Peru?

Leonard Possibly... Who knows. I do have to tell you I'm a very private person.

Harriet Private? (*She looks at a note*) It says here in your CV that you lived in a harem for three years.

Leonard That's what did it—I thought I'd joined a Turkish time share unit. Silly me.

Harriet Whereabouts exactly are you in Peru, Miss Banbury?

Leonard Please call me Myrtle. Do you know... (*He squirts the soda siphon across the mobile for sound effect*) On the coast of... (*Another squirt*) Not far from... (*One more squirt. The mobile gets wet*) It gets quite damp at this time of year.

They become disconnected

Dee Dee and Gus arrive at the front door

Leonard goes to the kitchen for a towel

Gus I've been ripped off... Whoever heard of VAT on a stripper... She was no dental student either.

Dee Dee Her flossing days are long over.
Gus And how dare her brother call me a daft old coffin-dodger.

Gus and Dee Dee enter the building. Leonard has pressed re-dial and again speaks on the phone as Myrtle

Leonard (*on the phone*) Hallo. Now where was I?
Harriet (*on the phone*) Exactly. Now I really do need to know how best to communicate with you.
Leonard Very sparingly.
Harriet What?
Leonard I'll be coming home soon to England.
Harriet So will you be staying with Mr Loftus?
Leonard Oh yes indeed, dear boy, I don't know how he puts up with an old lady like me who ... who ... who...

Dee Dee and Gus enter the flat—as Leonard becomes aware of them he is speechless, gasping into the receiver

Who ... who ... who... Oooh ... ah ... oh ... aah...
Harriet Hallo... Hallo, Myrtle, are you there? Myrtle, are you all right?
Dee Dee Dad, are you all right?
Gus What's happened?
Leonard Ah... Ah... Haaa...
Harriet Myrtle... Myrtle... Are you there...? Have you fainted...?
Leonard Aaaaaah... Aaaaaaah...
Harriet Put your head between your knees.

Dee Dee takes the phone from her father's hand

Dee Dee (*to Leonard*) Who is it?
Harriet Put your head between your knees—take a deep breath...

Dee Dee listens. Harriet is demonstrating by doing deep inhalations and long slow exhalations down the phone

Dee Dee Grampi. It is an obscene caller.
Gus (*eagerly*) Give it here.
Leonard Hang up, Dee Dee, hang up...
Harriet (*still heavily breathing*) In... And... Out...
Dee Dee You pervert... You sick old weirdo... You ought to have your goolies cut off...

Harriet is amazed. Gus takes the phone from Dee Dee

Gus 'Allo… 'Allo…
Harriet (*shouting desperately*) Er… Hallo… Dónde está la vieja señora…
Quiero hablar con Myrtle…
Gus (*playing the hero*) The rain in Spain stays mainly in the plain. (*He hangs up*)

Harriet sits puzzled in her office

Who the hell was that?
Dee Dee Yes, who was that?
Leonard A heavy breather.
Gus Yes, but they were heavy breathing in Spanish.
Leonard Were they? That's Brussels for you.
Dee Dee But Dad, it was you who was doing the heavy breathing.
Leonard Was I?
Gus You're not a heavy breather, are you?
Leonard No—certainly not.
Dee Dee You *were* heavy breathing, though.
Leonard I tell you, it's the only language those people understand.
Gus He sounded pretty depraved.

Harriet dials Leonard's home number on the land-line

Leonard I mean he was going… "Ooooh-Aaaah", so I answered him in no
uncertain terms… "Aaah-Ooooh" like that.
Gus You gave as good as you got, then.

The phone on Leonard's desk rings

Dee Dee (*into the phone*) Hallo…
Harriet Hallo. Is that Myrtle's nephew's house?
Dee Dee Do what?
Harriet Myrtle's nephew's house.
Dee Dee (*covering the phone*) There's a woman here speaking in code—it
must be for you, Grampi.
Gus (*eagerly taking the phone*) Hallo there, my little Lycra Queen… Dick
Turpin here. Stand and deliver.

Harriet is listening in speechless horror

Harriet Is that you again, Mr MacApple?
Gus Mr MacApple?
Harriet Shouldn't you be back in the hostel?

Gus The hostel? What are you talking about? I'm not going back there. Who
are you?

Harriet We spoke earlier.

Gus Did we?

Leonard is in a state of despair

Harriet Before Mr Loftus had you taken away.

Gus You mean my son?

Harriet (*placating him*) Yes, yes, of course, your son. Is he there? Can I have
a word with him?

Gus I think you'd better. (*He hands the phone to Leonard*) You are a horrible
little wart hog.

Gus and Dee Dee exit to the kitchen

Leonard (*into the phone*) Hallo... Hallo...

Harriet Mr Loftus, I'm extremely worried.

Leonard You're worried I'm demented.

Harriet Your aunt.

Leonard Myrtle, yes.

Harriet Sounded in a terrible condition—she needs TLC ASAP, OK?

Leonard How about HRT?

Harriet You look after her, Mr Loftus.

Leonard I will. I will.

Harriet Actually, there are one or two editorial notes I'd like to give her.

Leonard I'll pass them to her, don't worry. I am completely conversant with
my aunt's work—we're practically collaborators.

Harriet Are you indeed? Well, I'm afraid, in the event of Myrtle having had
any help with this manuscript the prize would be invalidated. We are a
feminist publishing house, Mr Loftus, our motto is For Women By
Women.

Leonard Is that "By" with an I or a Y?

Harriet Actually with an E as in "goodbye".

Leonard It was a joke.

Harriet I don't think so.

Leonard No, quite. Silly me. So where were we?

Harriet Well, the scene where Trevor takes Emily back to his flat is a bit
tame. It needs to be raunchier.

Leonard Raunchier? It's their first date, for God's sake. Trevor is a
gentleman...

Harriet Maybe, but he's not going to get very far banging on about his boring
old car, is he?

Leonard (*outraged*) It's a Morris Minor.

Harriet Boring. It needs spicing up. Readers today want a bit of action.

Leonard Don't we all?

Harriet I'm not saying I want the full rumpy pump on the first date.

Leonard I should hope not. Perhaps you could leave any other ideas on the answering machine.

Harriet I'm a very hands-on kind of editor.

Leonard I'm sorry to hear that.

Harriet Goodbye, Mr Loftus.

Leonard Goodbye, Miss Copeland.

Harriet ⎤
Leonard ⎦ (*together; hanging up*) Yuk. Yuk. Yuk.

Harriet leaves her office

Leonard sits at his desk and starts work

I'll show her. The silly old bag. (*Typing and reading*) "'Please go on,' Emily whispered, 'you were telling me about your Morris Minor.' Trevor gazed into her eyes. 'It's just a boring old car,' he said. 'Not the original two-door convertible 918 cc side-valve engine?' She could hardly believe that this was only their first date... 'No,' he murmured, 'One of the A series, the 803 cc overhead valve engine. Hard top.' Emily lay back with her eyes half closed. This was a man she could trust. 'Perfect,' she said with a sigh, 'Independent front suspension with rack and pinion steering. My favourite.' She was all his. They were kindred spirits. Trevor lent over and gently stroked her cheek." (*He chuckles to himself*) How do you like that, then? (*He activates the answering machine*)

Harriet (*on tape*) That scene is lovely now, Myrtle. Thanks. I still think it could get raunchier at the end.

Leonard Raunchier... (*He steels himself*) "Trevor lent over and kissed her briefly on the mouth". (*He activates the answering machine*)

Harriet (*on tape*) Raunchier.

Leonard Delete. Delete. "Trevor lent over and kissed her passionately on the mouth."

Harriet (*on tape*) Raunchier.

Leonard Oh God. Delete. Delete. (*He takes a deep breath*) Trevor kissed her passionately on the mouth and began to stroke her knee.

Harriet (*on tape*) Raunchier. Go on.

Leonard ...And began to stroke her thigh.

Harriet (*on tape*) More.

Leonard More...?

Harriet (*on tape*) Go for it, Myrtle.

Leonard ...OK ... he began to stroke her b-r-e-a-s-t. BREAST. Any advance on breast?

Harriet arrives at Leonard's front door carrying a briefcase and a bunch of flowers. She rings the bell

As usual, Leonard goes to the entryphone on automatic pilot

(*Into the speaker, as if to Gus*) Inside waistcoat pocket.

Harriet rings the bell again

(*Into the speaker*) How much do you owe the taxi, then?

Harriet (*into the entryphone*) Is that Leonard Loftus?

Leonard Yes. Who is that?

Harriet Harriet Copeland.

Leonard (*aghast*) Harriet Copeland... From...

Harriet Love Is All Around.

Leonard What? You're outside the front door, right? On my doorstep, right? You are paying me a surprise visit?

Harriet (*patiently*) That is astounding—was it intuition or did you work it out?

Leonard Oh ha-ha, Miss Copeland.

Harriet How's your aunt?

Leonard She's fine.

Harriet Still with you?

Leonard Yes... No...

Harriet Which?

Leonard Which what?

Harriet Yes or no?

Leonard She is asleep. She's got a sore throat. Pharyngitis, Laryngitis... She can't talk. Foot and mouth.

Harriet Can I come in for a moment?

Leonard I'm in the middle of cooking supper.

Harriet So?

Leonard A soufflé.

Harriet Lovely.

Leonard I've just got out of the shower. I haven't got a stitch on.

Harriet You don't sound very naked.

Leonard (*covering himself modestly*) Well, I am.

Harriet Mind you don't drip on your soufflé. Look, I just want to hand over the cash advance.

Leonard (*with no choice*) All right, then. It's the basement.

Harriet enters the building

Leonard rushes off and comes back with a bathcap on

He takes his jersey and/or shoes off and drapes a towel round his shoulders as the front doorbell rings. He shuts down the computer

(*Calling*) Hang on. Crabby bossy old cow—what does she have to come here for? (*He goes to the door to let Harriet in*)

She walks past him into the room. Leonard falls in love

How do you do?
Harriet How do you do?
Leonard You're not at all … at all … at all…
Harriet I'm sorry?
Leonard Tall… You're n-n-not at all tall.
Harriet Does it matter? Were you thinking of dancing?
Leonard N-n-no. I just thought you'd be…
Harriet What?
Leonard Different…
Harriet A crabby bossy old cow?
Leonard I'm so sorry.
Harriet Well, you're a very quick dresser.
Leonard No. Yes. (*Laughing inanely*) Very quick.
Harriet What's funny about that?
Leonard (*snatching off the bath hat*) Nothing. Nothing at all… Quick dressing is not funny at all.
Harriet (*presenting the flowers*) These are for Myrtle…
Leonard Lovely… W-w-would you like a drink? A glass of wine?
Harriet Thank you.
Leonard Red or white?
Harriet What have you got?
Leonard (*rushing to the kitchen*) Neither. Lucozade, Ribena, milk, Ovaltine, camomile, Listerine…

Harriet produces and opens a bottle of champagne

(*Producing two glasses*) A cup of tea … a glass of water?
Harriet You don't mind champagne?
Leonard I don't usually drink when I'm just here on my own.
Harriet On your own?
Leonard (*realizing the gaffe*) On my own chair, this chair. Auntie is asleep in there… (*He points to Dee Dee's room*) Obviously.

Harriet Poor dear—plenty of gargling.

Leonard What?

Harriet For her throat.

Leonard Oh yes, she'll be fine. Bless her. Cheers.

Harriet We had a long talk the other evening on the telephone.

Leonard I know you did. I was there.

Harriet She said you were out.

Leonard Ah yes... I was there and then I went out ... there I was and then there I wasn't—I was out there and when I came back she told me that you'd rung. There.

Harriet We just got chatting, woman to woman, the way you do...

Leonard Yes... She seemed to have enjoyed that.

Harriet What a life she's led.

Leonard Oh yes, she's quite a goer.

Harriet What?

Leonard Er... Goer to the theatre, goer to the opera, goer shopping...

Harriet She's just the kind of writer we need at Love Is All Around, a woman who's really been there.

Leonard Where?

Harriet A woman with real balls.

Leonard (*laughing nervously*) Definitely. I mean, that's what she writes with. Her work is full of them... Balls.

Harriet I found myself telling her all kinds of things.

Leonard I know you did.

Harriet She hasn't told you anything, has she?

Leonard About you and that bastard boyfriend of yours in Ruislip?

Harriet Yes.

Leonard No. No, certainly not—she's very discreet.

Harriet She's just one of those women you immediately feel easy with...

Leonard (*to himself*) Yes... It's funny that, isn't it?

Harriet She's very fond of you.

Leonard Yes, well, me of her too.

Harriet But you wouldn't tell her that of course, except in your Eggy-Peggy language.

Leonard Oh good Lord. That's private, just a family thing... I can't think why she told you about that.

Harriet Neggevegger meggind.

Leonard Veggery geggood. You're bi-lingual, then.

Harriet No, not really...

Slightly awkward pause

So you're a statistician?

Leonard Yes. It's not as boring as you'd think.

Harriet I'm sure it's not.

Leonard (*mesmerized by her*) Did you know, for instance, that the Lord's Prayer contains fifty-six words, the Ten Commandments two hundred and ninety-seven, the American Declaration of Independance three hundred and two and yet—here's what's interesting—the EU Directive on the export of duck eggs contains—guess.

Harriet I've no idea.

Leonard Twenty-six thousand, nine hundred and eleven.

Harriet Wow.

Leonard Exactly. I mean duck eggs...

Harriet So you've none of your aunt's creative talent, then?

Leonard No. It's probably skipped a generation. Maybe Dee Dee has it, though. I'm just Mr Boring.

Harriet Not at all.

Leonard I am.

Harriet No, you're not.

Leonard Yes, I am.

Harriet Well, just a bit perhaps.

There is another brief pause between them

(*Indicating the flowers*) Couldn't I just pop up and put these beside her bed?

Leonard No.

Harriet I wouldn't disturb her.

Leonard I think you would.

Harriet (*taking the contract etc. out*) I really do have to see her.

Leonard No, you don't—she is asleep.

Harriet I have to get her signature on this contract.

Leonard I'll sign it.

Harriet It has to be signed by Myrtle—in my presence. Then I can hand over the money.

Leonard (*scuppered*) Oh, isn't this just hunky-dory?

Harriet I could call back tomorrow. Maybe earlier.

Leonard No.

Harriet Later?

Leonard No... She needs a lot of sleep.

Harriet She'll be up soon anyway.

Leonard Will she?

Harriet For supper. Your soufflé.

After a moment's reflection Leonard realizes he is left with no choice. Inspiration comes to him

Leonard Right... Right. Well, I'll just pop up and consult with Auntie
Myrtle... You wait here. (*He turns on the intercom on the desk. Into the
intercom*) Hallo, Auntie... Auntie Myrtle... (*To Harriet*) Dead to the
world... (*He takes the flowers and goes up the stairs to Dee Dee's room*)
You'll be able to hear us on that. (*He knocks on the door*) Auntie... Auntie.

*Leonard enters the bedroom and starts using the intercom from off stage
to the sound of snoring, etc. and being both characters*

In the living-room, Harriet listens

(*Off*) Hallo, Auntie... (*Snore*) Auntie, it's me, Lenny... (*Snore*) I'm so
sorry to wake you. (*Snore*) Auntie... (*He kisses the back of his hand, as if
it is Myrtle. In Myrtle's voice, as if waking*) What... What is it? (*As himself*)
It's only me. Your Lenny-kins. I had to wake you. You see, Harriet
Copeland is here, she's come to visit you. (*As Myrtle, feebly*) Here?
Here...? Oh no, no, no. What a nerve... What does she want? (*As himself*)
She wants to witness you signing the contract for the book. (*As Myrtle,
choking a little*) She can't see me like this... I'm far too ... arrrrrgg! (*As
himself*) Oh Auntie, are you all right? (*He gently smacks his cheek*) Auntie,
it's not your weak heart, is it?

Harriet runs to the bedroom door in anguish

Harriet (*calling*) Mr Loftus—Mr Loftus...

Leonard emerges from the bedroom

Leonard Oh dear. I'm afraid she's having one of her turns.
Harriet No, no, please don't trouble her—just get her to sign it. I won't
intrude.
Leonard Very wise, Miss Copeland, very wise.
Harriet Please call me Harriet.
Leonard (*besotted*) Harriet.

Leonard returns to the bedroom

Gus arrives and enters the building

(*Off*) It's all right, Auntie, she's not coming up after all ... she just wants
you to sign this contract though, so that she can hand over the cash
advance... (*As Myrtle, breathlessly*) Thank the Lord... Well done. You are
a dear boy, a dear dear boy... Give me a kiss... (*A dreadful kissing noise*)

Gus enters the flat. Harrriet looks round at him. They do not know one another

Gus (*sexily*) Hallo.
Harriet Hallo.
Gus ...Have we...?
Harriet I don't think so.
Gus Splendid. Lovely. How do you do?
Harriet I'm Harriet Copeland.
Gus (*knowingly taps his chest*) The father.
Harriet (*horrified*) The father? How did you get in?
Gus (*holding up his key*) I'm a latch key pensioner. (*He laughs*) And you?
Harriet (*tapping her chest*) Visitor... I've been chatting to Leonard.
Gus My son.
Harriet Your son... Oh yes, he's told me all about you.
Gus Has he?
Harriet (*banging her chest*) Me Tarzan... (*She does the Tarzan cry*)
Gus Are you sure about that? Well, he never mentioned you. I've just got back from a murder weekend, you see, in Haywards Heath.
Harriet Have you indeed?
Gus Where is he?
Harriet He's in there with Myrtle Banbury.
Gus Of course he is. (*Beat*) Is this a game?
Harriet Sit down, Mr MacApple.
Gus Oh no, no, no, I'm not Mr MacApple...
Harriet I'm not accepting that.
Gus Suit yourself.
Harriet You're in denial.
Gus No, I am not.
Harriet Yes, you are.
Gus No, I am not.
Harriet (*forcefully*) Sit down, Mr MacApple.
Gus What is going on here?
Harriet Say "I am Mr MacApple".
Gus Why?
Harriet Come on now. Face the truth. Say it.
Gus (*bemused*) If it makes you happy (*like a robot*) I'm Mr MacApple.
Harriet Again.
Gus I'm Mr MacApple... I'm Mr MacApple.
Harriet Good... And Leonard Loftus isn't my son.
Gus Course he's not—his mother was a cantankerous old cow twice your age.
Harriet The truth is, Leonard wants nothing to do with you. You must go back where you belong.

Gus (*suddenly realizing*) To Birchampton… Oh, I see. I thought he wasn't serious.

Harriet Well, I'm afraid he was.

Gus looks miserably confused. From upstairs we hear Leonard winding up his charade and Harriet and Gus listen

Leonard (*off; as Myrtle*) And tell her I hope the end of Chapter One is sexy enough for her now. I'm afraid I'm a bit rusty on my rumpy pump. (*As himself*) Of course you are, Auntie. Suck another lozenge.

Leonard enters and becomes aware of his father with Harriet

(*Aghast*) Aaaah. What are you doing here?

Harriet Oh, thank God. He's got a key. But we have made some progress, haven't we, Mr MacApple?

Leonard What?

Gus (*seeking to oblige his son*) I'm Mr MacApple. I'm Mr MacApple, aren't I, Harriet?

Leonard Oh my God.

Gus (*like a robot*) I'm Mr MacApple. I'm Mr MacApple.

Leonard Tell me this isn't happening. Tell me I've walked in on an episode of *The X-Files*.

Gus That's the bad news. The good news is that this young lady is not your mother.

Harriet Shall I ring for the nurse?

Leonard There is no need, Harriet, this really is my father.

Harriet He lives here too?

Leonard For the time being. Yes.

Harriet So you're not Mr MacApple.

Gus (*nodding; like a robot*) I'm not Mr MacApple. I'm not Mr MacApple.

Harriet Good.

Gus (*inspired*) We're just one big happy family living here all together, aren't we, Lenny? With nobody moving out or anything. I'm sure it's what Myrtle wants and we mustn't forget Myrtle, must we?

Leonard No, of course, we mustn't. Dear Myrtle.

Gus How is she by the way? She sounded ever so poorly.

Leonard She is not ever so poorly. She's going to be fine. (*He hands Harriet the contract*)

Gus She's wonderful for her age.

Leonard She's got the constitution of an ox.

Gus That would be on your mother's side then.

Harriet (*handing over an envelope of money from her bag*) Well, there's the cash advance as agreed. Poor lady, is she really bankrupt?

Leonard (*putting the money in his pocket*) Oh yes, she got hit by the boom and bust cycle. Thank you.

Harriet I'm awfully sorry but I do have to get her signature on the receipt for that.

Leonard Do you?

Gus I'll take it to her.

Leonard No.

Gus It's time I got started on her blanket bath anyway.

Dee Dee arrives at the front door and enters

Harriet gathers her things

Leonard (*passing Gus*) There's no need.

Gus Well, actually, if you remember, she owes me some money. Quite a lot.

Leonard (*cottoning on*) She asked me to give it to you. She doesn't want disturbing what with one thing and another… (*He hands some twenty pound notes into Gus's hand*)

Gus And another.

Leonard And another. (*To Harriet*) I won't be a moment.

Harriet And once again give her my apologies for intruding.

Gus She doesn't mind, does she, Len? Go and kiss your aunt.

Harriet And tell her the sex was absolutely fine, this time, spot on.

Gus (*to Harriet*) It can be a bit hit and miss, can't it?

Leonard exits to the bedroom as Dee Dee enters the flat

Dee Dee Hi there, Grampi.

Gus I'm so glad you've arrived, I'd hate you to miss the fun.

Dee Dee (*kissing him*) What are you talking about? What are you up to?

Gus I'll come to that. (*To Harriet*) This is Dee Dee, my granddaughter.

Dee Dee How do you do?

Harriet How do you do?

They shake hands

So you're the one who has inherited your great aunt Myrtle's talent.

Dee Dee is baffled by the situation

Dee Dee Run that by me again.

Gus Your great aunt Myrtle. Upstairs.

Dee Dee My great aunt Myrtle? Have you been down the pub, Grampi?

Harriet Your father's up with her now.

Dee Dee Is he?

Harriet She's not well.

Gus Apparently she's a bit rusty on her rumpy pump but she's got the constitution of an ox, so not to worry.

Dee Dee What are you on, Grampi?

Leonard comes down stairs and is once again aghast to see his daughter home

Leonard Aaaaah. What are you doing here?

Gus She was worried about her great aunt Myrtle, weren't you, poppet?

Dee Dee nods, Gus shows her the twenty pound notes

Dee Dee Oh, yes, yes, of course.

Gus places one and then another twenty pound note in her hand. He then exits to Dee Dee's room

(*Cottoning on*) How is she, Dad, how is Auntie Myrtle?

Leonard (*handing over more twenty pound notes to her*) Fine. She's going to be fine. We'll soon have her on her feet again.

Dee Dee And again.

Leonard And again.

Harriet goes to the front door

You're not leaving?

Harriet I certainly am—after this, Big Brother would be a piece of cake.

They are interrupted by Gus on the intercom, pretending to be Myrtle

Gus (*off; as Myrtle*) Hallo, Lenny... Lenny...

Leonard (*after a moment of indecision; into the intercom*) Yes?

Gus (*off; as Myrtle*) Myrtle here—I just want to say you are not to send poor Gus to an old people's home...

They are all aghast as——

—*the* CURTAIN *falls*

ACT II

Two weeks later. Early evening

When the Lights come up, Dee Dee and Gus are dressed up ready to go out

Gus is possibly wearing a ghastly spangled waistcoat. The office of Love Is All Around is empty. Leonard is nowhere in sight. Dee Dee is helping Gus rehearse a karaoke version of You Make Me Feel So Young. *Gus is holding a furniture polish spray can as his microphone and is singing along to the soundtrack. Dee Dee is trying to make him do a kick or two and some other little dance steps, finishing up with Gus on one knee*

Dee Dee Brilliant... Victor Meldrew meets Shakin' Stevens.
Gus (*breathlessly*) I'm not sure about the big finish. I had a hernia not long ago.
Dee Dee Never mind, Grampi, think of the prize money.

Gus is now back on his feet but still holding the spray can—he uses it now as he talks to the audience

Gus Thank you, ladies and gentlemen. Actually, a funny thing happened on the way here this evening...
Dee Dee No, no, no...
Gus I met this Irishman...
Dee Dee No.
Gus Who bought a black and white dog because he thought the licence fee would be cheaper.
Dee Dee Stop, stop, stop... They do not want jokes.
Gus I said to the doctor I keep thinking I'm a pair of curtains and he said...
Dee Dee Pull yourself together.
Gus That's it.
Dee Dee Grampi, no jokes. Especially not very old ones. It's a karaoke competion—they don't want jokes.
Gus Oh, yes, they do.
Dee Dee Oh, no, they don't. With stuff like that, they'll disqualify you.
Gus Your father suggested I do "Wish Me Luck As You Wave Me Goodbye".

Dee Dee He was only joking. I wish he'd come, I don't know what's the matter with him.

Gus He's got the hots for that woman from the DSS.

Dee Dee Harriet Copeland?

Gus (*nodding*) I caught him listening to his old Dusty Springfield LPs at the weekend.

Dee Dee Oh dear, that is serious. You're right, he's gone all moody. (*She picks up a list from Leonard's folder and reads from it*) Look at this. "Things Women Do". What's all that about? It's pathetic at his age.

Gus (*a little crestfallen*) Yes, it is, pathetic. I'm afraid it's all part of his plan to get rid of me, I mean look at this pamphlet he's got from the surgery. (*He picks up the pamphlet off the desk*) "Are you looking after a confused elderly person in your home?" He's written underneath "I should coco". He wants to send me back to Birchampton.

Dee Dee To the twilight zone? (*She gives him a hug*) I thought they'd thrown you out.

Gus So did I, but they've got a new top security wing. It can't be helped your father has had enough of me.

Dee Dee (*sniffing*) What is that?

Gus Aftershave. It's called "Ride 'em Cowboy".

Dee Dee Gross.

Gus You gave it me last Christmas.

Dee Dee Actually, it rather suits you. (*She adjusts his tie*) Don't worry about Dad, he's just a bit tetchy.

Gus He's had the male menopause since he was thirteen.

Dee Dee Come on, we're going to be late. (*She collects coats etc.*) Now you promise no encores and no jokes, OK?

Gus OK... Now, glasses?

Dee Dee Breast pocket.

Gus Keys?

Dee Dee Top right inside.

Gus Wallet?

Dee Dee Hip.

Gus Money?

Dee Dee Leave it to me.

Gus We're off, then. He's not still in the bathroom, is he? (*He calls off*) Len— we're off. See you later.

Leonard (*off*) Bye, Dad. Got your glasses?

Gus Yeah.

Leonard Keys?

Gus Yeah.

Leonard Wallet?

Gus Yeah. I'm not senile, you know.

Dee Dee (*calling off*) Are you all right in there, Dad?

Gus leaves the flat

Leonard (*off*) I'm fine, darling. You just go and enjoy yourself.

Dee Dee takes a tenner from Leonard's wallet on the desk

(*Off*) Why don't you take a tenner from my wallet on the desk?
Dee Dee Oh Dad, thanks—you are sweet. (*She takes another ten pounds*)
Love you, Dad. Bye.

Dee Dee exits the flat. Turning lights off. Gus emerges onto the street

Leonard (*off*) No need to hurry home—enjoy yourselves.

Dee Dee joins Gus in the street

Gus You don't think, just for this evening, poppet, you could call me Gus.
Dee Dee Everyone will think you're a dirty old man.
Gus (*grinning*) Exactly, it pays to advertise.

Gus and Dee Dee go

*After a moment, the Lights come on and Leonard emerges. He is in full drag
including a shawl. He puts on his high heels, adjusts his wig etc. Perhaps
he wears glasses. He practises his feminity. He picks up the list of things
women do*

Leonard Let me see… They walk with small steps. (*He does*) They sit with
their legs crossed… (*He does*) …sometimes twice… (*He tries but can't*)
They smile a lot. (*He does*) They laugh inanely and fiddle with their hair
when they don't know what to say… (*He has a go*) They are for ever
checking their bottoms in the mirror… (*He does*) Why do they do that?
And they run their hands over their… (*He runs his hand over his breasts—
nothing there*) Oh my god…!

*Leonard runs off. He returns with two grapefruits as "breasts"—no good.
He settles for two tangerines which he inserts into his bra*

*Harriet arrives at the front door, carrying a small camera bag full of
equipment. She presses the entryphone button*

*The sound of it makes Leonard jump… He takes a final look in the mirror. He
will speak to Harriet with Myrtle's voice*

You are a very naughty woman. (*He goes to the entryphone*) Hallo...
Harriet Hallo, is that Myrtle?
Leonard (*wheezing*) Yes, my dear, do come in.
Harriet Thank you—I'm sorry I'm late.
Leonard (*pressing the button*) Not at all—let's be grateful for small mercies.

Before Harriet arrives at the flat door, Leonard has time to fetch the smoked salmon sandwiches from the kitchen and give himself a coquettish squirt of scent... Harriet knocks at the door and Leonard lets her in

Harriet How do you do?
Leonard How do you do?
Harriet At last.
Leonard What?
Harriet At last we meet. In the flesh.
Leonard (*with a girlish giggle*) I'd never be without it.
Harriet At the office we were having this joke that you didn't really exist.
Leonard (*laughing*) Oh, that is funny.
Harriet But here you are. (*She is scrutinising Myrtle*) You look wonderful...
    Much more...
Leonard What?
Harriet Robust than I expected.
Leonard (*a little indignant*) Robust... Robust indeed. I tell you I'm as frail
    as a newt.
Harriet You mean pissed.
Leonard How dare you.
Harriet No, no... Frail as a kitten. Pissed as a newt... It's the expression.
Leonard I know that. But newts can be frail too.
Harriet Yes, of course. Anyway, I'm so glad you're better.
Leonard Better?
Harriet Your throat, you look gorgeous anyway.
Leonard Pittle-pattle-poo, at my age. So do you.

A brief awkwardness

Now where would you like me?
Harriet Hmm?
Leonard For your camera—I thought here on the sofa... (*He strikes a pose
    with the shawl masking his face*) Like this...
Harriet Yes, well, something like that. (*She takes out her camera equipment,
    light meter, reflector, etc., and begins setting up*) Maybe not with the shawl
    in front of your face...
Leonard I'm such an old wreck—I hate having my picture taken.

Harriet I'm afraid that was the deal—it won't take long. It's a pity you haven't got any of your old photographs.

Leonard From my youth? Alas no. "The past unsighed for, and the future sure."

Harriet Wordsworth. Well, the CV you sent me was quite amazing. What an incredible life you've had.

Leonard Ah yes, I was quite a busy girl in my time.

Harriet How many husbands is it you've had?

Leonard You mean of my own... Seven. One less than poor old Zsa Zsa... Gabor. Widowed, divorced, annulled, divorced, widowed, divorced. Did a bunk.

Harriet Such a pity about all your photograph albums, I'd love to have seen a picture of you as a Bluebell girl...

Leonard Those were the days.

Harriet ...or when you were head prefect at Cheltenham Ladies' College.

Leonard Jolly hockey sticks. All burnt to a cinder I'm afraid—the Maharaja was a very jealous man. When I left him, he destroyed everything from my past.

Harriet What a bastard. Isn't that typical?

Leonard Exactly—men—who needs them?

Harriet Well, I do actually.

Leonard I say poppycock to men.

Harriet Do you?

Leonard Yes. Poppycock. Poppycock. Poppycock.

Harriet You're right—they're nothing but a lot of two-timing ratfink bastards, most of them.

Leonard Exactly, poppycock to the lot of them. So is there any particular two-timing ratfink bastard in your life at present, my dear?

Harriet No.

Leonard Good. Do you like champagne? I just happen to have a bottle on ice.

Harriet Leonard made me promise not to tire you out.

Leonard (*fetching the champagne*) Oh, he's a dear boy.

Harriet Where is he?

Leonard Er... He's down at the gym, working out. He's got a marvellous body.

Harriet (*surprised*) You wouldn't have thought so, would you?

Leonard Well, he has, as a matter of fact.

Harriet (*with her camera*) Hold it. Just like that... Lovely. You looked quite indignant.

All through this scene Leonard is fairly static and Harriet is moving around photographing him from all angles

Leonard Steady now. Not too close up, please.

Harriet You could have had a top class professional photographer, but Leonard said you wanted to have me.

Leonard (*entranced by her*) Oh, I do. I mean, did he?

Harriet He said you were a bit worried about your figure.

Leonard It's true—I am. I just hate it.

Harriet Me too.

Leonard You don't like my figure?

Harriet No, mine.

Leonard Yours. Yours is... (*He means "just divine"*)

Harriet I mean look at this... (*She points at her bum*) It's all that desk work.

Leonard It looks gorgeous to me—but then these are my reading glasses.

Harriet (*inviting him to feel it*) It's all flab—feel that...

Leonard No no, I couldn't really...

Harriet No, go on.

Leonard Well, all right... (*He feels the buttock*) Perfect... (*He feels the other buttock*) I mean perfectly robust... Now then, let's have some champagne.

Harriet In your day you must have been pretty junoesque.

Leonard D'you know... (*Juno*) I was. I was always big for my age.

Harriet That's what men go for. Big tits.

Leonard Not all of us. I mean not all of them—we just take what we can get, don't we? Pittle pattle poo to boobs. (*With a glass*) There we are.

Harriet Cheers. To women.

Leonard To women.

They drink

Harriet You know, sometimes, though, I wish I'd been born a man.

Leonard Do you? Well, it's not all it's cracked up to be... I imagine. I mean it can't be much fun always having to make the first move.

Harriet Is that such a problem?

Leonard For some men, I think it is.

Harriet Because they're shy?

Leonard Yes. It's not easy taking the initiative... Some things are just difficult to say.

Harriet What kind of things?

Leonard Oh... I don't know... Would you like another barley wine...? Or... Do you play table tennis? Or...

Harriet ...Do you fancy a shag?

Leonard I beg your pardon?

Harriet Hold it. (*She takes a photograph*) That's lovely over the top of your glass, like that... If only men would realise we're just as up for it as they are.

Leonard Are you? Are they? Are we?

Harriet Of course. Weren't you?

Leonard Er... Oh yes... Up it very for... Very up it for... Not so much now, of course.

Harriet But when you were my age, out in India, you must have had men after you in droves.

Leonard Oh yes, they were all over me like a rash. Polo matches, dinner parties, musical soirées, thé dansantes...

Harriet Balls?

Leonard No—it's true.

Harriet You must really know how to handle men.

Leonard (*coyly offering a sandwich*) In my own little way.

Harriet I've had so few really.

Leonard Sandwiches?

Harriet Men.

Leonard Oh good. I mean good ... sandwiches are hard to find, aren't they...? Just between ourselves... How many?

Harriet Sandwiches? Thousands.

Leonard No, how many lovers.

Harriet Let me see... Five... No... Six... Well, five and a half, technically speaking.

Leonard I don't think I want to hear the details. Especially not about the one with his decimal point missing.

Harriet It's not much of a score sheet for a girl of my age, is it? What about you?

Leonard Who's counting.

Harriet I mean my friend Linds says she's had the best part of thirty.

Leonard I wonder what she means by the best part?

Harriet Super... (*She takes a picture*) Can I just... (*She gestures to his hair*)

Leonard (*fixing it himself*) I'll do it. There. Not too close now.

Harriet I want to capture the real you.

Leonard That's what worries me.

Harriet They say the camera never lies.

Leonard I know they do.

Harriet That's lovely... Smile...

Leonard smiles grotesquely

No, maybe not... We're in a no-win situation as women, aren't we?

Leonard How do you mean?

Harriet Well, either we're branded as weak and feeble or we're fearsome and feminist. There's so much confrontation.

Leonard What ever happened to Vive là Difference? Perhaps we'd all be happier if we went back to the old days of men opening doors and women shaving their armpits.

Harriet Wow. You want to put us back in the kitchen baking fairy cakes and faking orgasms for king and country.

Leonard I'm just an old fashioned fuddy-duddy but it might be more popular than you think. There's nothing like a good fairy cake.

Harriet And what about sex? Have you never had to fake it?

Leonard (*out of his depth, laughing*) I wouldn't know how to begin.

Harriet That's what's so good about your book. Emily is a real heroine of today, a survivor like you. Men, what do they know, eh?

Leonard Exactly—I knew a man once who thought PMT was a pension fund.

Harriet What a prat. (*She winds on her film*) Nearly done. When is Leonard due home?

Leonard Later. Why?

Harriet I'd like to get one of the two of you together.

Leonard Oh, lovely. Sitting on Shergar next to Lord Lucan would be nice.

Harriet What do you mean?

Leonard He told you on the telephone he didn't want his photograph taken with me.

Harriet He didn't.

Leonard He did. I know he did.

Harriet How do you know?

Leonard I just do.

Harriet He said you were asleep when he called.

Leonard Well, I wasn't. Believe me, he will not have his photograph taken with me.

Harriet I see.

Leonard Nor me with him.

Harriet And I thought you two were so close.

Leonard We are, we are, we are ... inseparable.

Harriet (*the analyst*) I wonder. Tell me about him.

Leonard I can't.

Harriet Why not?

Leonard He wouldn't like it.

Harriet Please... He was married, wasn't he?

Leonard Oh yes, for fifteen years. Fifteen years and seven weeks.

Harriet And she walked out on him? He must be quite bitter.

Leonard No. No, I don't think so. He's not bitter. He just misses her, that's all...

Harriet Poor Lenny.

Leonard Yes, poor Lenny. He loved her, you see. He loved everything about her... (*In a reverie*).Her hair and her skin and the backs of her knees. The way she had of wrinkling her nose up when she was irritated with me...

Harriet What?

Leonard (*caught out*) Me ... me ... with my nephew.

Harriet As you say in your book. Love's a bummer.

Leonard Anyway, he wasn't quite what she wanted.

Harriet He was just too much of a wimp for her, was he?

Leonard I hadn't thought of that. I think she just wanted something more tempestuous, more exciting...

Harriet A swinging-from-the-chandelier kind of thing.

Leonard Not that easy with only an Anglepoise. (*A horrid realization*) Perhaps she just got tired of faking it.

Harriet Who can blame her.

Leonard She had Belgian blood in her, you see. Her grandmother was from Ostend.

Harriet (*taking one last shot*) Hold it. (*She takes it*) For a moment you looked so sad. You've got such lovely kind eyes.

Leonard Have I? So have you.

Harriet It's funny, isn't it, that a man like that with a wonderful extrovert of a father and you as an aunt should turn out to be so ... so...

Leonard Dull? You were going to say dull. Well, he's not, not inside. He's just not a man who wears his heart on his sleeve.

Harriet But he's obviously a marvellous father to Dee Dee.

Leonard Oh yes, and a marvellous son to Gus.

Harriet Hmm. How come he got custody by the way?

Leonard Nobody else would have him.

Harriet But working from home, he doesn't stand much chance of meeting anyone else.

Leonard He's always said he'll never fall in love again...

Harriet What? What were you going to say?

Leonard Oh, I'm just a dotty sentimental old bag and I'm afraid the champagne has gone straight to my head... But I have an idea that he finds you quite attractive.

Harriet (*laughing*) Me? Oh dear.

Leonard What's the matter?

Harriet Well, he's not quite my type.

Leonard There's no need to laugh.

Harriet I'm sorry.

Leonard What is your type anyway?

Harriet I've no idea. The type that's no good for me type, the "I'm afraid it's not going to work out and I'm going back to my wife in Ruislip" type... The bastard type.

Leonard Poppycock to him.

Harriet The trouble is my brain and my body can't seem to agree on what it is I'm looking for... My brain says "watch out this man has a neon sign over his head which says complete and utter bastard" and my body says "Who cares? Get 'em off." I'm not sure whose side I'm on.

Leonard Was it your brain then or your body that voted for the type who's not really your type, type.

Harriet It was a split decision—I think my body did a bit of ballot-rigging. It's history anyway.

Leonard You're in a bit of a muddle, are you?

Harriet I mean, why can't I be the me I am with you with him? The me I am with him is not at all the me I am with you.

Leonard Any you you are with me is fine with me.

Harriet It's odd, isn't it?

Leonard Why can't we be the people we like ourselves being. So what is it you're looking for?

Harriet I don't know... A Heathcliffe for my Cathy. An Antony for my Cleopatra...

Leonard A Darby for your Joan...

Harriet (*not flattered*) You're right, someone to tell you when there's spinach in your teeth, and your bum looks fine.

Leonard It does. It does... If you're too busy looking you might not even know when you've found him. (*Right under her nose*) He might be right under your nose.

Harriet I'll know, don't worry. I've always had this idea there'll be a—signal.

Leonard Is that a British Telecom thing?

Harriet Trumpets. Playing in my head. Haydn's Trumpet Concerto... Do you know it...? I always imagined, even as a little girl ... that I'd hear something like that, when he came along. Silly, isn't it?

Leonard No—not silly at all.

Harriet So tell me, what did Leonard say?

Leonard If he's not your type, what's the point?

Harriet Tell me anyway.

Leonard Well, let me see...

Harriet sits beside Leonard

He said you were beautiful ... very beautiful... He said that when he met you ... his heart leapt like... A tired old salmon in a highland pool.

Harriet Did he say that?

Leonard (*gazing at her*) More or less. He said that when your eyes met mine ... his ... yours... He felt...

Harriet (*involved*) What? What did he feel?

Leonard (*also very involved*) A kind of recognition, as though you'd belonged together, since the world began.

Harriet (*abstracted*) Len said that?

Leonard Yes. I think that was the gist of it.

Harriet Isn't it a pity he can't say those things for himself. Poor man.

Leonard He is who he is. Fine words butter no beans.

Harriet Isn't it parsnips?

Leonard Who cares? (*He gets up*) Still, it's quite beautiful, isn't it?

Harriet What?

Leonard Haydn's Trumpet Concerto. Have you finished?

Harriet Yes. I think I've got some lovely shots. Are we in for a happy ending, then?

Leonard (*tidying the champagne bottle*) I beg your pardon?

Harriet Emily and Trevor. Are they going to get together? You're not going to give me a sad ending, are you...? Go on. Tell me.

Leonard Happily ever after. I promise.

Leonard exits to the kitchen

Harriet You know what I think?

Leonard (*off*) What?

Harriet There's something fishy about the old aunt.

A humungous offstage crash

Leonard enters, panicked

Leonard Fishy? How do you mean?

Harriet I don't think she's quite what she seems. She's a little too enigmatic.

Leonard Maybe she is—maybe she isn't.

Harriet I wonder if she might turn out to be...

Leonard What?

Harriet A fake...

Leonard (*horrified*) In what way?

Harriet I can't put my finger on it.

Leonard Just as well. You'll just have to wait and see, won't you, you little minx.

Harriet Anyway, we're very excited about the book—it's going to be a real winner. We've got a huge promotion campaign lined up.

Leonard No, no, no... I told you—I can't, I won't do any of that sort of thing.

Harriet But Myrtle, you've no idea how vital it is.

Leonard Absolutely not. Having you here has already been... More than I can handle. I tell you I'm a very private *man—chester* United supporter and as such I cannot, I will not have anything to with that sort of thing.

During the following, Harriet follows the retreating Leonard into the kitchen

Harriet (*very appealing*) Oh, please, Myrtle, for me.
Leonard No.
Harriet I'd be there, all the time. At your side.
Leonard (*tempted*) No.
Harriet As one woman for another.
Leonard It's not a gender issue.
Harriet Come on.
Leonard No.
Harriet Please.
Leonard No.

While they are off stage, Gus arrives singing happily, at the front door. He luckily finds his key and enters

Harriet and Leonard enter as a continuation of the above

Harriet Just the Michael Parkinson show.
Leonard No.
Harriet Graham Norton?
Leonard No.
Harriet Richard and Judy?
Leonard I'd rather have open heart surgery done by an orangutan on speed.
Harriet Oh Myrtle, I need you.
Leonard Do you? Why don't you ask Leonard?
Harriet It's you I want.
Leonard Is it really?. Look, I tell you we think as one, Lenny and I.
Harriet But Myrtle, he just hasn't got your *je ne sais quoi*.
Leonard What's that?
Harriet I don't know.
Leonard It's odd that, isn't it? That he hasn't got my *je ne sais quoi*…

Gus enters the flat. As he opens the door, Leonard vanishes off upstage with the speed of summer lightning

Gus Hallo there.
Harriet Hallo.
Gus (*chuckling*) I'm not Mr MacApple.
Harriet (*banging on her chest Tarzan-like*) Me Tarzan. (*She does the cry*)
Gus What a muddle, eh? Is he here?
Harriet Lenny? No, he's down at the gym, working out.
Gus At the gym?
Harriet Yes.
Gus So what are you doing here?

Leonard enters with gusto

Leonard It's none of your business, Gus. Hattie and I have been having a business discussion…

Gus stands open-mouthed with amazement, Leonard circles him slowly, doing his best to carry on

…It's a private matter for the moment, isn't it, Hattie…? Our little secret. (*Defiantly*) Gus, I've told you before about leaving your mouth open—it makes you look half-witted.

Gus (*speechless*) Eeeee.

Leonard Close it.

Harriet Aren't you two on speaking terms?

Gus (*chuckling*) Of course we are—aren't we? So you two have got a little secret, have you?

Leonard Yes. We have, haven't we, Hattie?

Gus That's not the same little secret that you and I have got, is it, Myrtle?

Leonard No, it isn't.

Gus (*to Harriet*) I'll tell you mine if you tell me yours.

Harriet I'm in Myrtle's hands.

Gus Are you indeed?

Leonard Now Gus, where is Dee Dee?

Gus I left her with some friends. (*To Hattie*) We've been to a kedgeree competition.

Leonard He means karaoke.

Harriet Did you win?

Gus I came fourth in my group.

Harriet Well done.

Leonard In a group of how many?

Gus Four. It was my encore that let me down. I did *My Way*.

Leonard Your way?

Gus *My Way*, yes.

Leonard You did *My Way* your way?

Gus Yes.

Leonard You're lucky to be alive.

Gus (*to Harriet*) She's getting rather spiteful in her old age. Aren't you, dear…? (*Inspired*) Perhaps that's why Lenny is thinking of a retirement home.

Harriet What? It can't be true.

Leonard Of course it's not—Gus, have you been drinking?

Gus He hasn't dared tell you yet, Myrtle, dear. (*To Harriet*) The trouble is poor Lenny has a very low threshold of tolerance.

Leonard Lenny is a saint, I tell you.

Gus He has got a ruthless streak, though.

Harriet I don't believe it.

Gus We none of us like the idea, but it has to be faced.

Leonard No, it doesn't have to be faced, not now.

Gus (*truly in his stride*) Well, we'll have it out with Lenny himself when he comes back from the gym.

Leonard He won't be home for hours yet.

Gus No, no, he rang.

Leonard No, he didn't.

Gus (*showing the mobile*) Yes, yes, he did—I spoke to him. He's on his way.

Harriet He's coming after all?

Gus Yes.

Leonard No.

Gus (*to Harriet*) Could be interesting, don't you think? To see the two of them together.

Harriet (*to Leonard*) Yes, indeed. Who do you reckon he takes after?

Leonard It's difficult to say—he's a very handsome man.

Gus Do you think so?

Leonard (*bitterly*) On his mother's side.

Harriet (*to Leonard*) That would be your sister?

Leonard Er, yes.

Harriet (*to Gus*) Your wife?

Gus Er, yes.

Harriet It's such a pity. Are you sure I can't have a picture of all three of you together?

Gus Oooh, wouldn't that be just peachy.

Leonard No, it wouldn't.

Gus Myrtle, you're such a spoil-sport.

Leonard (*pushing him off*) Why don't you go to bed, Gus?

Gus Oh no—I haven't had such fun since I was strip-searched at Gatwick.

Harriet Actually, Myrtle was just telling me that she thinks Lenny is holding a bit of a candle for me.

Gus Oh! Isn't that *sweet*.

Leonard I shouldn't have told you—it's probably just wishful thinking on my part.

Gus Of course it is. I mean what would a beautiful girl like you want with a man like her.

Leonard Him.

Gus Her... Him.

Harriet Leonard. Actually, you'd be surprised. He's a man whose heart I can make leap like a tired old salmon in a Highland pool.

Gus (*mocking*) A tired old salmon... Oh, please.

Leonard Shut up, Gus. Harriet. You've no idea how happy it would make me.

Gus Me too. (*With renewed mischief*) I mean, look at the way he overcame his little problem—bless him.

Harriet What was that?

Leonard We don't want to hear.

Harriet I do.

Gus She does.

Leonard She doesn't.

Harriet Go on, Gus.

Gus Well, I'm sure there's nothing untoward in it, after all it was a long time ago, he was such a sweet little boy, it was probably just a silly childhood fad... (*He chuckles*)

Harriet For goodness' sake, what?

Gus Well, he had this thing about dressing up in women's clothes. Do you remember, Myrtle?

Leonard No, I don't.

Gus Oh, dear me, yes. I mean, it wasn't a fetish, not a fully fledged perversion—not then, when he was little.

Leonard I'm sure he's grown out of it now.

Gus Let's hope so. He was only a 32B in those days.

Harriet Poor little lamb.

Gus (*starting another scandal*) And as for his personal hygiene—I remember...

Leonard That's quite enough of your remembering. I just want to say one thing, Gus dear, I promise, I personally guarantee that while there's breath in my body there will be no question of any of us having to move out.

Gus No Birchampton? No twilight zone?

Leonard Absolutely not.

Gus You promise?

Leonard (*raising his hand*) Cubs' honour.

Gus Brownies.

Leonard And the British Legion.

Harriet Do you think Lenny will agree?

Gus Yes, do you think Lenny will agree?

Leonard Oh yes. Lenny knows what's good for him.

Gus (*gripping Leonard's hands*) You are a kind and wonderful woman.

Leonard (*gripping Gus's cheeks*) And you're just... Gus.

Harriet (*regarding this tender moment*) Aaaaah. Will you tell Dee Dee I've got some clothes off a fashion shoot she can have. Goodbye, Myrtle—I've so enjoyed meeting you.

Leonard And me you, my dear. It's been a pleasure.

Harriet I don't suppose I could persuade you to be my guest at the Woman of The Year luncheon?

Leonard I'm afraid not.
Harriet You don't approve?
Gus She doesn't qualify.
Leonard At heart I'm not really a woman's woman... What shall I tell Lenny
to do, then?
Gus I've got an idea.
Leonard Shut up.
Harriet Tell him... Tell him that faint heart ne'er won fair lady. Tell him to
ask me out to dinner. (*She offers her hand*) Goodbye.
Leonard Why don't you give an old lady a nice kiss?
Gus A question I've always found difficult to answer.
Harriet Of course.

They kiss—a slightly awkward moment

Leonard Goodbye.
Harriet (*going*) You hurry up now and let me have that happy ending.
Leonard I promise. Bye bye...

*Harriet leaves the flat. Leonard subsides from Myrtle's joyfulness into his
own gloom*

(*To Gus*) Don't say anything—not a word.

There is a long pause. Gus pours Leonard a large drink and gives it to him

Harriet leaves the building. She pauses, puzzled, then exits

Gus (*after a long pause*) In future I'd wear a darker lipstick if I were you.

Leonard sits despondently

Are you OK?

Leonard shakes his head

You're not OK?

Leonard nods

Would I be right in thinking that you're in a bit of a mess?

Leonard shakes his head

A hell of a mess?

Leonard shakes his head

A sodding great twenty-two carat, king-size, once-in-a-lifetime mess?

Leonard nods

Are you going to tell me about it or are we going to go on like this all night?
Leonard It's a long story.
Gus Oh, good.
Leonard And complicated.
Gus Surely not.
Leonard Do you remember when I was little I always wanted to write stories? Well, I've written a book, do you see? (*He takes out the tangerine that was his left "breast" and starts to peel it*) Or rather Myrtle Banbury has written a book, I had to use a pseudonym, do you understand? (*He offers a bit to Gus*)

Gus is disgusted by the idea

Love Is All Around is a feminist publishing house, you see? And now Harriet Copeland wants to publish it... She thinks I'm a woman.
Gus Well, I never.
Leonard ...And to make things worse. This is where it gets tricky.
Gus It was all so simple up to there.
Leonard Well... I always swore never again, didn't I? I'd never get involved again. But now I sort of rather think I might have ... er...
Gus Fallen in love?
Leonard Yes...
Gus Very well put.
Leonard Any ideas what I should do?
Gus You know I think I might have been a better father to you as a daughter.
Leonard We can't have a relationship based on a lie. I've got to confess, haven't I, Dad?
Gus Steady now, there's no need to panic.
Leonard It's my only option, isn't it, the truth?
Gus I've never tried it. In my experience the truth is over-rated rather like aromatherapy or sun-dried tomatoes.
Leonard It has to be faced, though—I mean, it can't go on like this, can it?
Gus Not unless she's a gender-bender too.

Dee Dee comes to the front door with a carrier bag—she enters

In the living-room Gus and Leonard are pondering

Leonard In any event, I'm snookered.
Gus How do you mean?
Leonard I'm caught between the Trades Descriptions Act and Sexual Discrimination.
Gus Plus the frock is overdue on its rental. Take her out to dinner. Chat her up.
Leonard I've forgotten how.
Gus It's like riding a bicycle.
Leonard You're talking to a man with a buckled crossbar.
Gus (*embracing his son*) Come here.

Dee Dee enters the flat

> *Without hesitating, Gus and Leonard go into a brief but intricate tango routine that takes Leonard off to the kitchen with a flourish of her shawl*

Gus turns casually to his granddaughter

Dee Dee So you pulled, then.
Gus Hi there, Poppit.
Dee Dee What is it, Shag-A-Granny week?
Gus She's very shy… (*He calls off*) Milky with two sugar, please, Conchita.
Dee Dee So where's Dad?
Gus Down at the gym.
Dee Dee What gym?
Gus Any gym. Please, will you go to bed.
Dee Dee Actually, you won a prize after all. (*She removes from the carrier bag a foot-high statue, a replica of the road sign of the two old people with walking sticks crossing the road*) The Golden Oldie award.
Gus I'm very flattered.
Dee Dee I warned you not to do an encore.
Gus They wanted *My Way*. They were shouting for it.
Dee Dee They were shouting "Go Away".
Gus Go to bed, you horrible girl, I'll explain everything in the morning.
Dee Dee You don't have to, Grampi, I'm not stupid. And you can tell Conchita in there that he promised he'd drive me to school in the morning.
Gus (*amazed*) Eh?

The Lights fade in the living-room and come up in Harriet's office. It is a few days later. The phone rings

> *Harriet enters and answers it*

Harriet (*into the phone*) Hi Linds—thanks for callimg back, I'm in crisis.
... Yes, yes, of course it's a man. ... No, that's the trouble, he's not a bastard
at all... I mean, I'm the girl who goes for mean matcho high-fliers in
Armani suits, right? ... Exactly, the Rolls Royce syndrome—so how come
I'm considering a Robin Reliant? What do I think I'm thinking about
thinking about a rather shy dowdy statistician? What's he like? He's
somehwere between a Trainspotter and Basil Fawlty. What's happening
to me, Linds, have my hormones broken down? Or do I need a sabbatical
at Club Med? I mean, this is a man I wouldn't look at twice normally. What
do you think I should do? ... Look at him twice—thank you very much...

There is a knock on her office door

Come in.

Leonard enters, carrying a bunch of roses and an umbrella

(*Into the phone*) I'll call you right back... Goodbye. (*She hangs up*)
Leonard I'm sorry to disturb you.
Harriet Lenny, come in. I was just reading your aunt's last chapter—it's
quite marvellous. Do sit down.
Leonard (*putting his stuff down*) So this is your office...
Harriet Er ... yes. I'm sorry I missed you the other evening. You were at the
gym.
Leonard No, I wasn't at the gym.
Harriet Oh?
Leonard I lied, you see. I don't work out. I've never been to a gym.
Harriet Who cares?
Leonard I just wanted to set the record straight. My body is not at all
marvellous.
Harriet I'm sure it isn't. Is that why you came to see me?
Leonard Not altogether. I'm afraid I've got some rather bad news for you.
Harriet Bad news?
Leonard About my aunt.
Harriet Is she all right?
Leonard She's gone.
Harriet Gone? Gone where?
Leonard I don't know—she's just disappeared.
Harriet Oh my God.
Leonard She said she didn't think she could go through with it, the book,
the whole thing.
Harriet I can't believe it. Why didn't you stop her?
Leonard I went to take her her tea this morning and she'd gone.

Harriet Did she take anything with her? Clothes? Passport? Moisturiser?

Leonard The lot. There's no trace of her. (*He takes out a letter*) She left this note for you. Here.

Harriet (*taking and opening it*) Oh, the poor darling. You don't think it's my fault, do you?

Leonard No, no, not at all. I think she liked you.

Harriet Poor darling... (*She opens the letter*) Imagine at her age having an identity crisis. I can't read her writing, it's a bit wobbly. Would you...?

Leonard (*reading*) "My dear Harriet, by now you will have heard of my decision, not taken lightly, to withdraw from our arrangement. I'm sure you'll think me very selfish in letting you down like this and I am so sad that we shall not meet again..."

Harriet is looking out the window and Leonard is clearly not actually reading—he knows it by heart

"I'm just a silly old woman who doesn't really deserve your interest and concern."

Harriet No, no, you're not...

Leonard (*as if still reading*) Yes, yes, I am... "I'm a fraud—not worthy of your approval. Believe me I'm nowhere near as profound as you imagine—deep down inside I'm superficial to the bone... Meeting you the other night and seeing in your... (*He gazes into her eyes*) beautiful limpid blue/grey/brown eyes all that faith you placed in me, made me realize that I can't go on... I've had a long talk about this to Lenny. He is such a dear, kind, sympathetic, intelligent, witty and yet caring and perceptive boy and he has done his best to dissuade me..."

Harriet Did you really?

Leonard I did, I did... "But I am resolute. Thank you so much for the happiness, the rare happiness you brought me."

Harriet is very moved

"I hope you find some for yourself one of these days. Dear Harriet, listen carefully, I'm sure you'll hear those trumpets one day."

Harriet (*quietly*) Haydn's *Trumpet Concerto*. Do you know it?

Leonard No... "I enclose a cheque to refund my advance payment... Please don't think unkindly of me. With many fond memories, yours ever, Myrtle."

Harriet I must go after her immediately and find her.

Leonard "PS: Do not come after me immediately and find me."

Harriet Oh, the poor darling. I'm going to miss her terribly.

Leonard Me too.

Harriet (*looking at the cheque*) This cheque is from you, on your account.
Leonard Er... Yes. She gave all the money to me.
Harriet She wanted you to have a life.
Leonard Yes... She did, didn't she? I'm afraid I'm rather a disappointment to her...
Harriet I don't think so.

Pause

So that's it, then?
Leonard Yes, I just came to deliver the cheque and the letter from Myrtle.
Harriet And those lovely roses.
Leonard (*in the doorway*) No, actually, they're from ... m-m...
Harriet You?
Leonard Yes... Yes, they are... Bye.

Leonard goes, leaving his umbrella

Harriet Bye...

The phone rings and she picks it up

(*Into the phone; frustrated*) Hallo. Love Is Nowhere To Be Found... Hi, Linds ... yes, yes, it was ... no, he didn't... Not even a teensy weensy little hint... No, Linds, I do not want to meet you in the wine...

Leonard enters

Leonard Sorry to interrupt.
Harriet (*not hanging up*) You weren't. What is it?

A brief pause and then he picks up his umbrella

Leonard Er... I forgot my brolly. Sorry.

Leonard leaves again

Harriet Of course you did—you forgot your brolly. (*Into the phone*) Linds, I'll see you there in ten minutes.

Harriet hangs up and exits

The Lights cross-fade into the living-room area. It is empty

Dee Dee (*off; on the intercom*) Grampi... Grampi... Where have you got to...? Are you there?

Gus enters from the kitchen with a beer

Gus Yes, yes, here I am... It's thirsty work this overloading business...

Dee Dee (*off*) Down, Grampi, downloading... Where have you got to?

Gus Page two hundred and thirty-seven... (*At the computer*) They've just arrived at the hotel...

Dee Dee (*off*) I'm coming down. I don't want Dad to catch us...

Gus (*speed reading*) "...Trevor threw Emily over his shoulder..." That's the stuff... "mahogany four-poster"...

Dee Dee enters

Dee Dee Hurry up, scroll down, Grampi, scroll down...

Gus Sounds like a folk song... There we are... "flickering candle-light ... blonde hair on the pillow ... bla, bla, bla ... pleasure ... knickers off..."

Dee Dee Gross.

Gus I should think so... (*Reading*) "'Yes yes yes,' Emily moaned ... bla bla bla shooting stars" ... bla bla ... earth moved kind of mallarky et cetera et cetera... Way hay ... loverly jubberly.

Dee Dee Pull yourself together, Grampi.

Gus He's a dark horse, your father, I never knew he had it in him. A proper little Danielle Steel on the quiet.

Dee Dee What's strange is that Dad can be so good at all that sort of stuff on paper and yet...

Gus ...So useless in the flesh. It's just the practical he needs to work on.

Dee Dee I do wish I'd seen him in your Miss Marple kit.

Gus He looked a treat... What am I saying? He looked like Gordon Brown in drag.

Dee Dee No stammering, no rapid blinking, no hyperventilating?

Gus Not a trace, a proper little extrovert. A bit like in Cyrano.

Dee Dee Where's that, Grampi? The real choker is having to hand back all that dosh.

At the front door, Harriet arrives, carrying a bag and presses the entryphone button

Gus Don't tell me he's lost his keys.

Dee Dee (*into the entryphone*) Hallo.

Harriet Hallo. Dee Dee? It's me, Harriet. Can I come in a moment?

Dee Dee Of course. (*She presses the button*)

Harriet enters the building. Gus and Dee Dee tidy up a bit

I wonder what she's after.

Gus Maybe she wants to borrow a frock off your father. Where the hell is he anyway, it's unlike him to go AWOL.

Dee Dee You don't think he's gone on a bender?

Gus (*in an impersonation of Humphrey Bogart*) Give me another Lucozade, barman, and a packet of low fat crisps.

Dee Dee (*at the computer*) I think she's cool.

Gus You don't think she fancies me, do you?

Harriet knocks and Gus opens the door

Come in.

Dee Dee Hi.

Harriet Don't worry, I'm not staying—I'm on a double yellow, just across the road.

Gus Would you like something to drink?

Harriet No, thanks.

Dee Dee Dad's not here, I'm afraid.

Gus It's Myrtle you're looking for, I expect?

Harriet Well, yes and no. Actually, I'd like to see them both.

Gus
Dee Dee } (*together*) Aah.

Harriet Together.

Gus
Dee Dee } (*together*) Together.

Harriet I think it would be interesting to get them face to face across a table.

Gus
Dee Dee } (*together*) Yes, that would be interesting.

Harriet There are things between them they need to resolve... I think it would help them both, don't you?

Gus Yes, yes, I do.

Dee Dee I'm afraid Dad too has done a runner.

Harriet Why? Is there something troubling him?

Gus You mean like how to ask you for a date.

Dee Dee He wants to, I know he does.

Gus Yes, yes, he does. Very much.

Harriet Then don't you think he should mention it to me?

Dee Dee He really does have the hots for you.

Gus Well, the lukewarms, anyway.

Harriet If only he had his aunt's flair for words.

Gus Yes indeed. We've just finished the book.

Dee Dee I think it's brill... Who could imagine that Dad...

Gus kicks her

(*Recovering*) ...could have an aunt who had such a talent for that kind of stuff.

Gus I liked that bit where Emily and Trevor are playing hunt the thimble in the jacuzzi...

Dee Dee Grampi, get a grip.

Harriet I just wish I could talk to her—persuade her to let us publish it. (*She hands a bag to Dee Dee*) I nearly forgot—these are for you, a few T-shirts. (*She takes them out one by one*) Black, black, black ... and—black.

Dee Dee All my favourite colours.

Harriet Exactly.

Dee Dee Thank you... Thank you very much.

Harriet It's nothing ... my pleasure. We just had them at the office. So you don't think they're together, then, Myrtle and Leonard?

Gus No, not as such.

Harriet They could be at opposite ends of the country, then.

Gus That would be very uncomfortable.

Leonard warily approaches the entryphone and presses the button

Harriet You don't seem very concerned.

Leonard and Dee Dee talk through the entryphone

Dee Dee (*answering the entryphone*) Hallo?

Leonard (*confidentially*) Dee Dee? Don't say anything. It's me, Dad.

Dee Dee Yup.

Leonard Is that Harriet's car across the road?

Dee Dee Yup.

Leonard Is she in there with you?

Dee Dee Yup.

Leonard Looking for me?

Dee Dee Yup.

Leonard Looking for Myrtle?

Dee Dee Yup.

Leonard Looking for both of us?

Dee Dee Yup.

Leonard (*to himself*) Well, sod this for a game of soldiers.

Dee Dee Yup.

Leonard I should speak to her, shouldn't I?

Dee Dee Yup.

Leonard You think I haven't got the bottle, don't you?

Dee Dee Yup.

Leonard Well, I haven't. I'll wait out here till she's gone. OK?
Gus Who is it?
Dee Dee (*to Gus*) RSPCA. (*Into the entryphone*) Quite right. A dog is for life, not just for Christmas. (*She hangs up*)

Leonard sits on the doorstep, pondering. Gus is looking round, then has an inspired thought

Gus Hang on a mo'… I've got an idea… Where's the mobile?
Dee Dee I haven't got it. Dad must have taken it.
Gus (*dialling on the landline*) Exactly, either him *or*… Myrtle.
Dee Dee Myrtle?
Gus One of them must have it.
Harriet Good thinking.
Dee Dee Oh yes, of course. Brill…

Suddenly the mobile rings in Leonard's pocket. Flustered, he takes it out and answers it. He and Gus speak into their phones

Leonard (*on the phone*) Hallo.
Gus (*on the phone*) Hallo. Is that you, Myrtle?
Leonard It's me, Dad. What are you talking about?
Gus *Oh, Myrtle dear*, we've all been so worried about you…
Leonard What…?
Gus (*he feigns listening*) Yes, yes, we're all fine. Missing you, of course.
Leonard Leave me alone, you daft old bugger.
Gus (*chuckling*) Bless you too, Myrtle, my dear.
Leonard You are supposed to be on my side, for God's sake, now get rid of her.
Gus Harriet? As a matter of fact she wants a word with you, too.
Leonard No, no, no, no…
Gus Oh yes, yes, yes.
Leonard I'll kill you.
Gus Love you too, Myrtle. I'll just pass you over… Here she is…

Gus passes the phone to Harriet, who will take up the phone conversation. Leonard will speak to her with Myrtle's voice

Leonard Dad, please don't…
Harriet Hallo… Hallo… Myrtle…
Leonard (*reluctantly as Myrtle*) Hallo…
Harriet Myrtle, are you all right?
Leonard I'm fine, thank you, fine…

Harriet Lenny gave me your letter. I'm so sad that it all had to end like this.
  I so enjoyed meeting you.
Leonard And me you.
Harriet I've got some lovely photographs.
Leonard Have you?
Harriet Please, please tell me where you are.

*Willie Briggs, a schoolboy/pensioner/football-fan/maniac or ASM, who
lives in a neighbouring flat enters from the front door. He naturally
overhears the following speech and listens in amazement*

Leonard Well, if you must know, dear, I'm at my little hide-away up here
  in the Hebrides... As I told you I'm a recluse... Just a dotty old woman
  who's perfectly happy alone here on this wild deserted beach... The sea
  wind blowing in my face, and the waves lapping over my feet... (*Aside to
  Willie*) Bog off.
Harriet What was that?
Leonard (*gesturing Willie to leave*) Seagull.

Willie Briggs leaves

Harriet Oh Myrtle, can't I persuade you to come back?
Leonard Please don't.
Harriet It's not because of Lenny, is it? You don't think he's jealous?
Leonard Good Lord, no.
Harriet I just wish to God we could find him. He's gone missing.
Leonard I know... I mean... Oh dear. Probably best to leave him alone. Gus
  and Dee Dee can manage.
Harriet Actually, it's me... I want to see him.
Leonard Do you?

Dee Dee gets up, pours a large brandy and quietly leaves the flat

Harriet Yes. I think between us, you and I could help him to open up a bit,
  the way you can, for instance... He needs to tap into his feminine side.
Leonard I'm not sure that's such a good idea.

*Dee Dee appears beside her father on the doorstep. He is very glad of the
drink*

Dee Dee What's going on, Dad?
Leonard (*aside*) I don't know, darling. (*He drinks*) I'm a very tired, worried
  old woman.
Dee Dee You're a man.

Harriet Hallo... Hallo...

Leonard (*into the mobile, accidentally*) I'm a woman.

Harriet Of course you are.

Leonard Hold on.

Dee Dee Come on, Dad—where's your stiff upper lip?

Leonard One of them is quivering here on the doorstep and the other one is in the Outer bloody Hebrides... Oh, what a tangled web we weave when first we jump into women's clothing...

Harriet Hallo, hallo—what's going on?

Leonard (*needing time to think*) Hold on a moment will you, my dear... Er ... There's a chap here having a spot of trouble with his caber...

Harriet Hallo. Hallo... Are you all right? (*To Gus*) She's helping someone with their caber.

Gus Not tossing, I hope, at her age.

Leonard has an inspiration. He covers the mobile and then presses the entryphone button. It sounds in the flat

Dee Dee What are you doing?

Leonard Nothing ventured nothing gained.

Gus (*going to answer the entryphone*) Who the hell can that be? Not the RSPCA again. (*Into the entryphone*) I hate dogs.

Gus and Leonard speak to each other through the entryphone

Leonard Hallo.

Gus Hallo.

Harriet (*into the phone*) Hallo... Hallo...

Leonard (*as Myrtle, into the mobile, nearly caught out*) Hallo. Hold on, for God's sake.

Gus Hallo. Who is it?

Leonard (*passing the mobile to Dee Dee*) It's me, Dad.

Gus Lenny?

Leonard I think so. I want to talk to Harriet.

Gus What...? You can't. She's on the telephone to Myrtle.

Leonard Dad, believe me, I know she is. Tell her I want a word with her.

Gus You're bonkers, that's what you are.

Leonard I'm working on it.

Gus (*to Harriet*) Harriet—I've got Lenny here. He's at the front door, he wants to talk to you.

Harriet What...? Right... Good. (*Harriet speaks into the phone before going to the entryphone*) Hallo... Hallo, Myrtle... Myrtle...

Leonard (*as Myrtle; into the phone; flustered*) Hallo. Yes?

Harriet (*into the phone*) Hold on, will you, I've got Lenny on the
   entryphone, he's come home…
Leonard (*as Myrtle; into the phone*) Oh, how marvellous—you go ahead.

*Harriet passes the phone to Gus and Gus passes her the entryphone handset.
Outside, Leonard passes the mobile to Dee Dee and concentrates on the
entryphone. Leonard and Harriet talk through the entryphone*

Harriet Hallo.
Leonard Hallo.
Gus (*into the phone*)Hallo.
Dee Dee (*into the mobile*) Hallo.

****Bear with this. It really does work.*** These four hallos can be repeated
if necessary, on a good night*

Gus (*into the phone*) What is going on?
Dee Dee (*into the mobile*) I don't know, Grampi, Dad's doing an audition
   for *Blind Date*.

There is a pause—nobody seems to know who should speak

Harriet Well?
Leonard Fine, thanks. And you?
Harriet Have you got anything to say to me?
Leonard Er … no. It's a bit chilly…
Harriet You are an exasperating man.
Leonard So I gather. Apparently fifty-eight per cent…
Harriet Shut up. Look, I really want your aunt to let me publish her book.
   So I need to get the two of you together, face to face.
Leonard You can be pretty exasperating yourself. (*Another inspiration*)
   Look… Hold on a minute. (*He takes the mobile from Dee Dee. To Dee
   Dee*) I've got the answer.
Dee Dee What was the question?

Leonard, as Myrtle, speaks to Gus over the phones

Leonard Hallo, Gus, Myrtle here.
Gus I give up. I'm going back to Birchampton.
Leonard I've decided to let Harriet publish my book after all.
Gus Are you serious?
Leonard Yes. Will you tell her.
Gus Of course I will. (*To Harriet*) Harriet, Myrtle says she's changed her
   mind, you can go ahead with the book.

Harriet Oh, that's marvellous.
Leonard On the condition that I can have absolute privacy.
Gus Fine, I'll tell her.

Leonard hands the mobile back to Dee Dee

(*To Harriet*) Dear Myrtle says she must have her privacy…
Harriet Sure, that's OK. I understand.
Gus (*into the phone; fabricating*) What? Oh no, Myrtle… (*Over-acting*)
You can't … that's outrageous… Harriet won't like that at all… All right,
I'll tell her.
Harriet What is it?
Gus (*to Harriet*) I'm afraid Myrtle says she wants more money.
Harriet What?
Gus More money.
Harriet How much?
Gus (*into the phone; to Dee Dee*) How much?
Dee Dee (*into the mobile; nonplussed*) Grampi, what the hell are you up to?
Gus (*into the phone; ignoring her*) I see… I'll tell her. (*To Harriet*) Double.
Harriet Double… Bloody hell.

Leonard and Harriet talk through the entryphone

Leonard What's going on?
Harriet Apparently your aunt wants more money.
Leonard Oh God. How much?
Harriet ⎱ (*together*) Double.
Dee Dee ⎰
Harriet (*to Gus*) I can't.
Gus (*into the phone*) She says she can't.
Dee Dee (*to Leonard*) She says she can't.
Leonard (*to Dee Dee*) She needn't.
Dee Dee (*into the mobile*) She needn't.
Gus (*to Harriet*) She says you must.
Harriet (*into the entryphone*) She says I must.
Leonard (*into the entryphone*) You don't have to.
Harriet (*into the entryphone*) Yes, I do. (*To Gus*) I will.
Gus You'll pay?
Harriet I have no choice.
Gus Myrtle drives a hard bargain.
Harriet But she's worth it.
Gus (*into the phone*) Hallo, Myrtle? Harriet has agreed to pay, isn't that
wonderful?
Dee Dee (*into the mobile*) Grampi, you're a greedy conniving crook.

Gus (*into the phone*) I'm doing my best.

Harriet (*to Gus*) What's she saying?

Gus (*to Harriet*) I think dear Myrtle is rather overcome.

Leonard (*into the entryphone*) What's she saying now?

Harriet (*into the entryphone*) She's overcome.

Leonard (*to Dee Dee*) She's overcome.

Dee Dee (*into the mobile*) I'm overcome, am I, Grampi?

Gus (*into the phone*) Shut up.

Harriet (*into the entryphone*) Thank goodness that's settled.

Leonard (*into the entryphone*) Yes indeed.

Harriet (*into the entryphone*) Hold on a minute. (*To Gus, taking the phone from him*) May I? (*Into the phone*) Hallo… Hallo… Myrtle…

Dee Dee is in panic at hearing this

Dee Dee (*urgently*) Dad… Dad.

Leonard hurriedly takes the mobile phone and talks to Harriet, as Myrtle

Leonard Hallo… Hallo… Harriet.

Harriet Are you all right?

Leonard I'm a bit overcome…

Harriet I'm so pleased about the book.

Leonard Now then, how's my nephew?

Harriet You know Lenny.

Leonard Oh yes. Still on the doorstep, I suppose?

Harriet Of course. (*The analyst again*) You know, Myrtle, I think he needs to know you love him.

Leonard I do. I do.

Harriet And likewise him you.

Leonard He does. He does.

Harriet You both need to hear it. That's my whole point. Hold on… (*She takes the entryphone from Gus and gives him the phone*) Lenny? Lenny?

Now Leonard and Harriet talk through the entryphone

Leonard (*as himself; panicked*) Yes? Hallo.

Harriet Lenny—do you love your aunt?

Leonard Yes, yes, of course.

Harriet Tell her, for God's sake, tell her.

Leonard (*befuddled with a phone in each hand*) How? I don't know where she is.

Harriet Hold on. Don't go away. (*To Gus*) Pass me the telephone.

Gus passes her the phone

Thank you.

Harriet now has both phones, one in each hand, as does Leonard. He is Myrtle on the mobile and himself on the entryphone

(*Into the entryphone*) Tell her... (*Into the phone*) Tell him. (*She holds the two handsets together, head to toe as it were, in front of her*)

Leonard (*into the entryphone*) I love you, Auntie. (*Into the mobile, as Myrtle*) I love you, Lenny.

Harriet (*to both receivers*) And you trust one another.

Leonard (*into the mobile, as Myrtle*) I trust you, Lenny.

Leonard (*into the entryphone*) I trust you, Auntie.

Harriet (*to Gus*) Ahh... That was nice. (*Into the phone*) Wasn't that lovely?

With an apparatus to each ear Leonard isn't sure in which ear he heard that

Leonard (*into the mobile, as Myrtle*) Er ... yes. Now you get off the telephone, my dear girl, and get on with your life.

Harriet I'll be in touch.

Leonard (*into the mobile*) No, no, no. Absolutely not. I think we both know that. You take care of yourself and watch out for those trumpets.

Harriet hangs up the phone, and talks to Leonard through the entryphone

Harriet Hallo, hallo. Lenny?

Leonard I'm still here.

Harriet Wasn't that lovely? It should have cleared the air.

Leonard It certainly has.

Harriet So... Tell me...

Leonard What? Tell you what?

Harriet (*kindly*) Tell me a statistic or two...

Leonard (*into the entryphone*) Oh right. Did you know, for instance, that thirty-seven per cent of all adult male statisticians who are single parents living in rented basement flats with their wayward daughters and their cantankerous old fathers find it very difficult to...

Harriet hands the entryphone to Gus and tiptoes out of the flat

Dee Dee (*urging him on*) Go on—go on, Dad.

Leonard (*funking it*) To ... keep up with all the washing.

Dee Dee Tell her in Eggy-Peggy, Dad.

Leonard (*into the entryphone*) …EggI theggink eggI eggam…
Gus (*into the entryphone*) I no speakee da language… (*He hangs up*)

Harriet, unseen by Leonard, appears behind him on the doorstep

Harriet You were saying…?
Leonard (*very surprised to see her*) I was just saying what diffficulty some
    people have in saying things…
Harriet What kind of things?
Leonard (*fluently*) Things like: You really do make my heart leap like a tired
    old salmon…
Harriet In a highland pool.
Leonard That kind of thing, yes. You've got the most beautiful eyes in the
    world and you've absolutely no idea how much I want to take you in my
    arms…
Dee Dee (*impressed and disgusted*) I don't believe this.
Leonard (*to Dee Dee*) Clear off.
Harriet Why don't you?
Leonard What?
Harriet Take me in your arms…
Leonard Because first I have to make a confession.
Harriet Oh, please, not the truth—not now.
Leonard There is no Myrtle Banbury. I have no aunt. I invented her.
Harriet (*with cod surprise*) Good heavens—I don't believe it, she gasped,
    it can't be true.
Leonard I tell you, I'm a greedy unscrupulous fraudulent double-dealing
    cross-dressing cheat.

The sound of Haydn's Trumpet Concerto *fades in*

Harriet Nobody's perfect.

*As the music swells, they kiss. An optional extra as they kiss is that two heart-
shaped sets of lights appear or pink lights start flashing round about them*

CURTAIN

FURNITURE AND PROPERTY LIST

Further dressing may be added at the director's discretion

ACT I

On stage: STREET ENTRANCE:
Lamp-post
Entryphone

LIVING-ROOM:
Entryphone
Desk. *On it*: computer, fax, answering machine, intercom
Chairs
Waste-paper basket
Coffee table. *On it*: cup of coffee
Soda siphon
Cordless phone
Transistor radio (practical)
2 glasses
Mirror
Landing chest (near stairs)

HARRIET'S OFFICE:
Wall charts
Chair
Desk. *On it*: tidy stationery, note, pile of manuscripts
Waste-paper basket

Off stage: Manuscript, ironing, letter (**Leonard**)
School things, mouth spray, cigarette (**Dee Dee**)
Can of Coke, packet of crisps (**Leonard**)
Shopping bag. *In it*: spotted dick on plate under cling film, dress, huge
   bra (**Gus**)
Mobile phone (**Dee Dee**)
Bunch of flowers, briefcase. *In it*: contract, envelope of money, bottle
   of champagne (**Harriet**)
Towel (**Lenny**)

Personal: **Dee Dee:** Walkman
                 Harriet: watch (worn throughout)
                 Gus: baseball cap, key, glasses, mobile phone
                 Leonard: money
                 Leonard: bathcap

ACT II

Set: Living-room:
                 Furniture polish spray can
                 Pamphlet on desk
                 2 ten pound notes in **Leonard**'s wallet on desk
                 Bottle of scent
                 Champagne

Off stage: 2 grapefruits, 2 tangerines (**Leonard**)
                 Small camera bag. *In it*: camera, light meter, reflector (**Harriet**)
                 Smoked salmon sandwiches (**Leonard**)
                 Mobile (**Gus**)
                 Carrier bag. *In it*: foot-high replica road sign of two old people with
                     walking sticks (**Dee Dee**)
                 Bunch of roses (**Leonard**)
                 Brolly (**Leonard**)
                 Beer (**Gus**)
                 Bag. *In it*: black T-shirts (**Harriet**)
                 Six-pack of lager (**Willie Briggs**)

Personal: **Leonard:** wig, glasses, shawl, letter, mobile phone

LIGHTING PLOT

Property fittings required: street lamp
1 composite set: living-room, office, street. The same throughout

ACT I

To open: General lighting concentrated on **Harriet**'s office

Cue 1   **Harriet**: "...which I am returning..."   (Page 1)
            Cross-fade to **Leonard**

Cue 2   **Leonard** exits   (Page 2)
            Cross-fade to **Harriet**

Cue 3   **Harriet**: "This is actually rather good..."   (Page 2)
            Cross-fade to **Leonard**

Cue 4   **Leonard** puts can of Coke and crisps on table   (Page 3)
            Cross-fade to **Harriet**

Cue 5   **Harriet**: "Myrtle Banbury..."   (Page 3)
            Cross-fade to **Leonard**

Cue 6   **Leonard**: "There we are."   (Page 4)
            Bring up lights on **Harriet**

Cue 7   **Harriet** exits   (Page 4)
            Fade office lights down

Cue 8   **Leonard**: "...towards Emily and whispered...""   (Page 14)
            Bring up lights on **Harriet**

Cue 9   **Leonard** and **Harriet** both hang up   (Page 17)
            Fade office lights down

Cue 10   **Harriet** enters   (Page 18)
            Bring up lights on **Harriet**

Cue 11   **Harriet** leaves   (Page 23)
             Fade office lights down

ACT II

To open: General lighting, evening outside

Cue 12   **Dee Dee** exits, turning lights off in flat   (Page 35)
             Fade lights in flat

Cue 13   **Leonard** enters, switching lights on in flat   (Page 35)
             Bring up lighting in flat

Cue 14   **Gus**: "Eh?"   (Page 50)
             Fade lights in living-room, bring up lights in office

Cue 15   **Harriet** exits   (Page 53)
             Cross-fade to living-room area

Cue 16   **Leonard** and **Harriet** kiss   (Page 64)
             Heart-shaped lights flashing round them (optional)

EFFECTS PLOT

ACT I

Cue 1   **Harriet**: "…by Myrtle Banbury."   (Page 2)
Phone rings in office

Cue 2   **Gus** rings entryphone   (Page 9)
Entryphone rings

Cue 3   **Gus** rings entryphone   (Page 9)
Entryphone rings

Cue 4   **Leonard**: "Is this a conspiracy?"   (Page 13)
Mobile phone rings

Cue 5   **Harriet**: "…shagging by the Inglenook."   (Page 14)
*Phone rings on **Leonard**'s desk*

Cue 6   **Leonard** is about to replace receiver   (Page 15)
Leonard's *phone rings*

Cue 7   **Gus** and **Dee Dee** exit   (Page 18)
Phone rings in office

Cue 8   **Leonard** twiddles transistor radio dial   (Page 19)
Transistor radio noises

Cue 9   **Gus**: "You gave as good as you got, then."   (Page 21)
*Phone on **Leonard**'s desk rings*

Cue 10   **Leonard** activates answering machine   (Page 23)
Harriet *on tape as script page 23*

Cue 11   **Leonard** activates answering machine   (Page 23)
Harriet *on tape as script page 23*

Cue 12   **Leonard**: "…kissed her passionately on the mouth."   (Page 23)
Harriet *on tape as script page 23*

Cue 13	**Leonard**: "…began to stroke her knee." **Harriet** *on tape as script page 23*	(Page 23)
Cue 14	**Leonard**: "…And began to stroke her thigh." **Harriet** *on tape as script page 23*	(Page 23)
Cue 15	**Leonard**: "More?" **Harriet** *on tape as script page 24*	(Page 24)
Cue 16	**Harriet** rings entryphone *Entryphone rings*	(Page 24)
Cue 17	**Harriet** rings entryphone *Entryphone rings*	(Page 24)
Cue 18	**Leonard** drapes towel round his shoulders *Doorbell rings*	(Page 25)

ACT II

Cue 19	As Curtain rises *Karaoke song plays, cut when ready*	(Page 33)
Cue 20	**Harriet** rings entryphone *Entryphone rings*	(Page 35)
Cue 21	**Harriet**: "…something fishy about the old aunt." *Huge crash in kitchen*	(Page 43)
Cue 22	Lights come up in office *Office phone rings*	(Page 50)
Cue 23	**Harriet**: "Bye…" *Office phone rings*	(Page 53)
Cue 24	**Harriet** rings entryphone *Entryphone rings*	(Page 54)
Cue 25	**Leonard** rings entryphone *Entryphone rings*	(Page 56)
Cue 26	**Dee Dee**: "Brill…" *Mobile in **Leonard**'s pocket rings*	(Page 57)

Cue 27	**Leonard** rings entryphone *Entryphone rings*	(Page 59)
Cue 28	**Leonard**: "…double-dealing cross-dressing cheat." *Fade in Haydn's* Trumpet Concerto	(Page 64)
Cue 29	**Leonard** and **Harriet** kiss *Swell Haydn's* Trumpet Concerto *to fill theatre*	(Page 64)

MADE AND PRINTED IN GREAT BRITAIN BY
LATIMER TREND & COMPANY LTD PLYMOUTH
MADE IN ENGLAND